TAKING
STOCK

TAKING STOCK

A Spiritual Guide to Rising Above Life's Financial Ups and Downs

Rabbi Benjamin Blech

Foreword by Monsignor James P. Lisante

AMACOM

American Management Association
New York • Atlanta • Brussels • Chicago • Mexico City • San Francisco
Shanghai • Tokyo • Toronto • Washington, D.C.

Special discounts on bulk quantities of AMACOM books are available to corporations, professional associations, and other organizations. For details, contact Special Sales Department, AMACOM, a division of American Management Association, 1601 Broadway, New York, NY 10019.
Tel.: 212-903-8316. Fax: 212-903-8083.
Web site: www.amacombooks.org

Library of Congress Cataloging-in-Publication Data

Blech, Benjamin.
    Taking stock : a spiritual guide to rising above life's financial ups and downs / Benjamin Blech; foreword by James P. Lisante.—1st ed.
        p.   cm.
    Includes bibliographical references and index.
    ISBN 0-8144-0787-0
    1. Investments—Psychological aspects.   2. Stocks—Psychological aspects.   3. Finance, Personal.   I. Title.

HG4515.15.B58   2003
332.024—dc21

                                        2003008506

Printing number

10   9   8   7   6   5   4   3   2   1

With the love that only a father can have for his son,
I dedicate this book to Ari—
who never stopped helping, advising, editing, and
adding his creative talents.

Contents

Foreword

One of the great paradoxes is how much time and energy we must devote in this life to acquiring something that is of no value in the life to come-whether we conceive of this future life as the memories that our loved ones have of us, or as our own personal immortality. Money, which seems an indispensable companion in the here and now, must be left behind at the border of the grave.

And never did money seem more indispensable than in America at the end of the twentieth century. The remarkable stock market of the late 1990s held out the promise of wealth for nearly everyone who could take advantage of it-with the encouragement of those seemingly "in the know." People who never before expected such prosperity in their lives began to take their good fortune for granted. Our society, which has always had a strong tendency to equate value with price, seemed more wealth obsessed than ever.

Now, the first years of a new century bring the cold light of dawn and the realization that there is no such thing as a risk-free investment or an ever-climbing stock market. For many, especially the relatively inexperienced new investor, this has come not merely as a disappointment, but as a life-altering experience. All kinds of plans-from starting a family to preparing for retirement-have been put on hold. No wonder many people feel seriously disoriented.

Rabbi Blech tells us that he shares this experience first-hand, and so understands very well what others are going through along with himself. But, as he makes abundantly clear in this book, he has a remaining wealth to share. It is a wealth of knowledge and insight that comes from his immersion in the wisdom of a great spiritual and religious tradition. He draws from it lessons of enormous value for himself, as well as for others whose lives have gone through this dislocation.

From the Bible, the thoughts of sages from many ages, the findings of research, and the experiences of people he knows or has read about, Rabbi Blech has put together a persuasive case for putting wealth in its proper perspective. For all the time and energy so many expend in pursuing, its place is, in reality, far from the center of what is most important in living a worthwhile life, and there are few people sadder than those who mistake their worth as human beings for the value of their portfolios.

My own religious tradition agrees, as the figure of the "rich young man" in the Bible shows. Anxious to do the right thing, he cannot face the challenge of giving up his possessions to help the poor. He walks away sorrowful because the right thing costs too much in terms of this world's good. As Rabbi Blech points out, many have made this same choice and found disappointment instead of peace.

This is a remarkably easy and genial book to read, but it is not one whose insights will be completely grasped after one reading. *Taking Stock* is a book to return to and to think about again and again. While the economic crisis that inspired it will pass, the value of its message is permanent.

—Monsignor James P. Lisante

Preface

I have a close personal friend who just barely survived the worst year of his life. Depressed, perplexed, almost totally hopeless—he even wondered on occasion whether his life was still worth living.

What overwhelmed him so was not the loss of a loved one. His spouse was still alive, his children healthy. Although I had never known him to be obsessed with money, it was the almost unprecedented decline of the Dow Jones and Nasdaq that was the source of his misery. He was one more victim of the crash, a crash that left him financially bruised, psychologically battered.

To understand his pain requires some knowledge of his background. He is a highly respected professional who has spent his life involved with education and community service. By the standards of his field, he has received adequate compensation—enough to raise a family of six in middle-class comfort. But then came a turning point that abruptly changed his life.

Retiring in his mid-sixties, my friend began to invest in the market. With an unexpected golden touch, or so it seemed, he showed his genius for picking stocks. It was the booming last years of the last century and nothing ever went wrong. Penny stocks ran up to $100 valuations. Venture capital investments made him a millionaire several times over. The Internet and dot-com purchases brought him wealth beyond his wildest dreams. It wasn't difficult for him to plan what he would do with this unexpected blessing. He would give lots to charity, take exciting trips, support his children and grandchildren, and secure the future of his entire family—all this was now possible. And then it wasn't. Far more quickly than the money came, it all disappeared!

Day by day, the blood letting continued. When it seemed his stocks could go no lower (and he certainly couldn't sell them then!), they did, and the phrase "new year-end lows" was as apt a description of his moods as of his portfolio prices.

For a time, I hardly recognized him. His trademark smile was nowhere to be seen, a bubbling and enthusiastic personality all but disappeared. It seemed almost incredible to watch a person of strong intelligence as well as religious belief fall apart so completely.

Have you already guessed by this time that my friend is none other than me? Yes, after years spent as rabbi of a congregation as well as professor at Yeshiva University, I rode the roller coaster of wealth to the top and then hopelessly and frighteningly careened to the bottom.

How ironic! After preaching and teaching the value of spirituality over materialism ("Don't succumb to the golden calf"), I was as bothered by losing money as anyone. I wanted to use my wealth to do good, I rationalized. I was another Tevye in a new version of *Fiddler on the Roof,* asking God to make me a rich man . . . again.

Loss is a tragedy, even when what we've lost is "only money." The most pious, the most religious, the most spiritual human being has a right to feel deep personal sadness at a time of dramatic change of fortune. And I was deeply sad.

But in the aftermath of this personal bout with depression, I have some wonderful news to share with you. It is perhaps the "happy ending" to the story—and the reason I have written this book. I knew I had to get well, to once again become the confident, contented, and complete person I was before. Go to a therapist? I could no longer see myself spending the hundreds of dollars that would cost. Besides, had I not helped so many people in the past by counseling them?

Of course, it's so much harder to make yourself realize what you can glibly convey as truth to others. To paraphrase Mel Brooks, the difference between minor surgery and major surgery is that the former is an operation performed on other people, the latter on oneself. But even the major surgery of self-healing can be accomplished. I know it because I did it. I came out of my depression because I meditated on the values, ideas, and ideals that find a place in the writings of the wisest of all people of every faith.

Taking Stock is the result of my own personal odyssey. It's not meant to be autobiographical. It should help you to know, though, that this book was written by someone who has suffered just as you have—and was able to find the way back to peace of mind and personal well-being. Although I'm a rabbi, this is not a Jewish book by any means. It's a self-help book, universally relevant, with insights that I hope will change your life, as they did mine.

This is a relatively small book with a large agenda. It can offer you the inspiration as well as the emotional and intellectual approach you need to deal with financial crisis.

This book is meant to be read more than once. It's a guide for you to review—not simply until you *understand* its message but until you truly *believe* it as well.

Benjamin Blech

Acknowledgments

The greatest lesson about wealth that I've learned in my life is this simple truth: No one is so rich that he can do without a friend.

Money is the way most people measure their success. I've come to the realization that there is no poverty greater than loneliness, no riches more satisfying than the blessings of friendship.

Knowing that makes me realize that I am probably one of the wealthiest people on earth. Every day, I thank God for the gift of so many people who surround me with their love, their caring, and their unstinting willingness to be of help in every possible way.

This book is testimony to the kindness of a wide circle of friends who read the manuscript in progress, who offered constructive suggestions (and, yes, even criticisms), who lifted me up when I felt down and—perhaps most important of all—who inspired me to believe that my words could change the lives of millions of readers.

Out of many, I must single out a few friends who made especially significant contributions: Andrew Steinerman, Yitz Grossman, Paul Stark, Dr. Henry Lieberman, Rabbi Mitchel Wohlberg, Rabbi Simeon Schreiber, Mark Karstaedt, Sid Taubenfeld, Andy Krasnow, Meira Gross, Debra Rudolph, as well as the very distinguished roster of nationally prominent figures who blessed me with their most gracious comments that appear on the cover.

Thanks to my agent, Gene Brissie, for all of his efforts as

well as for guiding me to AMACOM, who must have the nicest people in the world of publishing. I treasure the talents, the efficiency, and the friendship of all those I've worked with—particularly Jacqueline Flynn, Mike Sivilli, and Niels Buessem.

Last on this page but first in my heart is my wife Elaine, who allowed me to always feel bullish about life, even in those dark days when the bear ruled.

Benjamin Blech

TAKING STOCK

Introduction

Walk into any gathering and within minutes talk will turn to the state of the economy. People are troubled as they have never been before. Layoffs have replaced job security. Investments made years ago that held the promise of early retirement have shrunk to a fraction of their former value. Some of the "most successful" corporations have filed for bankruptcy, bringing down with them the fortunes of many hapless workers and investors. Small wonder that consumer confidence has plummeted and more and more Americans are worried about their financial futures.

A leading indicator of these economic woes has been the dreadful performance of the stock market over these past few years. Current figures indicate that *since the highs of 2000, the market has wiped out almost $7.5 trillion of stock values*—a staggering sum that cuts into the pockets of over *150 million Americans*! I am one of these Americans and in all probability you are too.

Investors today include construction workers and waiters, mechanics and butchers, professors and high-school students. As Peter Lynch, the highly successful Fidelity Fund manager, wrote in his best-selling book, *Beating the Street*, "I actually heard cabdrivers recommending calls and barbers bragging about how they'd bought options." With the turn of the century, we personally witnessed what Bernard Baruch many decades ago taught us should always serve as the very best market

1

indicator: "When shoeshine boys are buying, it's time for you to sell."

According to recent statistics, 61 percent of U.S. families have money invested in the stock market—in individually directed retirement accounts, in mutual funds, or in individual shares.[1] Almost all of us have been affected by the 90 percent plus declines of the much-touted "stocks you *must* own" that financial gurus like "Money Honey" Maria Bartiromo at CNBC (**C**ommentary **N**ow, **B**ankruptcy **C**oming) kept assuring us would continue to skyrocket. Small wonder that almost all of us, confronting today's new realities, are searching for a spiritual, psychological, and emotional "lifeline," an approach that enables us to get by, and a philosophy that can help us to move on.

I believe I have found this perspective; it worked for me, and it will work for you. Other books promise to teach you how to invest, how to make money in even the toughest of markets, how to "beat Wall Street." This book is for those who have—at least temporarily—been battered by the street that any New York cabbie can tell you goes only one way and leads into the river!

As a survivor, I've written this for all of us who must now try to cope with the loss of what we've grown up believing is the sole key to happiness. I draw on a wealth of insights from religious teachings of all faiths, combined with contemporary findings by psychologists, sociologists, and profound thinkers. The topic is serious, but the style is light, accessible, and filled with illustrations and anecdotes.

The goal is to find answers to the most meaningful questions, to make sense out of the apparent unfairness of life, to discover how to go on when life doesn't seem to be worth living. This book will inspire you. This book will comfort you. This book will make you think. Read it and read it again. Let it help you the way its insights helped me. My promise to you is that for a fraction of what it would cost you to be healed by a therapist you will learn that life, even after you've lost millions, is not only worth living—it's worth treasuring.

Note

1. *Forward Observer*, January/February 2002.

CHAPTER 1

Say Goodbye–
It's Really Gone

That money talks

I'll not deny

I heard it once

It said, "Goodbye."

—Richard Armour,
British author

Far too many times in my life I have had to face the difficult task of informing someone that his or her loved one—a mate, a parent, a child—had just passed away.

Invariably, the response was the same: "It can't be! That's impossible. He was well just a while ago. I spoke to her only yesterday on the telephone. It was just last week that we went out together. . . ."

Strange when you think about it: We all know that we are mortal. From the day of birth we draw inexorably closer to the day of death. Yet our first reaction to its occurrence is always denial.

Denial is the first way we attempt to deal with a change of circumstance we are afraid to confront. That concept, as I will soon show you, is as true when people lose money as when they lose loved ones.

5

We Die in Stages

When Elizabeth Kubler-Ross was an assistant professor of psychiatry at Chicago's Billings Hospital, she came to realize that there was one area in modern medical care that was completely ignored. While the terminally ill were kept alive longer than ever before, almost no attention was paid to the care of the dying. When she began to give seminars on death and dying, the field of study was so new that a word had to be coined: "thanatology," from the Greek *thanos* (dead).

One of the important discoveries she made has relevance to the living as well. After working with hundreds of terminally ill patients, Dr. Kubler-Ross realized that physically, emotionally, and intellectually, death is not a moment but a process. In fact, there are distinct and clearly identifiable stages—denial, bargaining, anger, depression, and finally acceptance—that almost every patient goes through. The first stage, denial, is that "it can't happen to me!"

Denial Has Consequences

For both the dying and the grieving families after death, denial has dramatic and damaging consequences. Carl Jung, one of the founders of modern psychology, put it well when he said: "We cannot change anything until we accept it." The one who doubts he is truly sick will never seek the serious treatment he desperately needs in order to get well. The mourners who refuse to accept that their loved one is gone will leave the room of the deceased intact, fantasize daily about their relationship, and never allow the grieving process to run its course to acceptance and eventual consolation.

Denial and the Dow

This book isn't about death, but it *is* about loss. In Hebrew, interestingly enough, the word for "money" is the same as the word for "blood" (the Hebrew word is *damim)*. We give our blood and our sweat to earn enough for our families. It isn't too harsh a comparison to say that losing a fortune in the stock market is almost like a mini-death. A part of our efforts and dreams has just gone down the drain. That's probably why according to Jewish tradition "an impoverished person is considered as if he is dead."

I don't have to tell you that in the wake of the market crash we have many walking corpses in our midst. Unfortunately, they too follow the path so clearly outlined by Dr. Kubler-Ross.

Two years ago your stock traded at over $100 a share. Today it sells for pennies. "That's impossible," you continue to say—just as you have been saying throughout its precipitous drop to these all-time lows. Denial stopped you from acting rationally. Denial prevented you from admitting that your original purchase was a mistake. And denial will allow you to watch incredulously as the company for which you got such a great tip is slowly sinking into bankruptcy.

Admit it. Your stock is worth a lot less than it was. Accept the new reality. Then you will be able to move on. Repeat to yourself as a mantra the words I quoted before in the name of Carl Jung: "We cannot change anything until we accept it."

Your portfolio is only worth what it's worth now, not what it was worth yesterday. Can't bear to look at the numbers? Prefer to live with the fantasy of insane Internet company valuations and the madness of a bull market based on hype and herd mentality? Fantasies may seem appealing—but woe to the person who confuses them with reality.

The law of gravity was kind enough to reveal itself to Sir Isaac Newton with the thud of an apple on his head. Yet even this great genius admitted, in the aftermath of his foolish participation in the investment craze for shares in the spurious South Sea Company, "I can calculate the motions of heavenly bodies, but not the madness of people."

Denial isn't going to help you cope with the Dow or with any of your other financial problems. Loss—whether it's your money, your job, or your most valued possession—doesn't disappear just because you say it didn't happen. The ostrich with its head in the sand hasn't found a solution; he's just going to remain stuck in the same rut until he decides the time has come to face reality.

Remember This Prayer
The famous theologian of the last century, Reinhold Niebuhr, wrote "The Serenity Prayer" that has helped millions of people throughout the world:

> God, give us grace to accept with serenity the things that cannot be changed, courage to change the things which should be changed, and the wisdom to distinguish the one from the other.

What cannot be changed already *is* a reality. Wishing won't make your bank account bigger, the Nasdaq jump higher, or help the Dow Jones recapture its previous levels. Of course, there are things you can change: you'd be foolish to let your financial misfortunes paralyze you into total passivity. You do have the wisdom to distinguish one from the other. The fact that the economy is down doesn't mean that *you* have to be, too. Don't spend all your time looking backwards. It's much healthier—and more rewarding—to move forward.

Can I at Least Cry?
I know it's easy to say, "Get over it." But it isn't easy to do. So God gave us a way to recover. Remarkably enough, what philosophers and religious teachers of old considered a great gift is all too often today held in disrepute. When Adam and Eve were expelled from the Garden of Eden, they couldn't bear the thought of losing Paradise. That, according to ancient legend, was when God gave human beings the ability to shed tears in order to wash away the unbearable hardships of life.

"Real men don't cry," goes a popular saying. What a stupid statement! What would they suggest as an ideal alternative to weeping? Carry the pain inside of you so that it never leaves?

Allow everything to remain bottled up until it can no longer be contained and explodes in violent fury?

Once, I performed a funeral for a young man whose young wife was left with three small children to raise. The widow's composure was astonishing, and everyone remarked on it favorably: "Look, how she held back her tears." "Thank God, she didn't create a scene." No sobbing or wailing, not a single hysterical outburst. Yet just three months later, I had to extensively counsel the very same person, now a zombie-like figure bent on self-destruction, robbed of the blessing of simple outpourings of emotion. The ancients were wiser. Jeremiah did not consider it beneath his prophetic dignity to pray, "Oh, that my head were waters, mine eyes a fountain of tears." King David readily confessed in his Psalms, "I melt away my couch with tears."

Admitting is the start of healing, and tears are a gift. What is it about our value system that makes crying a crime and the show of feelings a failing? I can't be sure of the cause. But I know that as a result we pay the price in incalculable pain and suffering.

Can we possibly expect someone to cope with a loss he has not yet been forced to acknowledge?

It is the tragedy of our times that we consider nature's way of healing a weakness, even as we continue to confuse emotion with immaturity. What I mourn in our age is the unnatural contempt for natural manifestations of emotion.

So cry, please cry, about either one of the *damim*, blood or money. And then move on to another chapter—in this book and in your life.

— What You Want to Remember —

- Denial is the worst way to deal with your problems.

- Acceptance allows you to move forward—not to live in the past but to lay the foundation for a far better future.

- Don't feel ashamed for caring so much about the loss of your money. You're justified in feeling sad—just don't be depressed (and I'll help you with that in the forthcoming chapters).

- If you need to give expression to your sadness, don't be afraid to have a good cry.

- Most important of all: Don't diminish the significance of these insights by describing them as simple and obvious. Try to repeat to yourself every morning this profound observation of German poet and philosopher Johann von Goethe: "All truly wise thoughts have been thought already thousands of times; but to make them truly ours, we must think them over again honestly, till they take root in our personal experience."

CHAPTER 2

No, You're Not Stupid

Bachelors' wives and old maids'
children are always perfect.

—Nicolas Chamfort,
eighteenth-century French author

There's a famous story about Winston Churchill who was confronted one night in the House of Commons by a Miss Bessie Braddock, a socialist member from Liverpool. With a smile, she turned to Churchill and said, "Winston, you're drunk!" Churchill instantly replied, "And you, Madam, are ugly. But tomorrow morning, *I* shall be sober." It's always better to have a fault that can disappear than one you'll be stuck with forever.

Losing money is temporary. You can always make it back. But being stupid is a lifelong condition. (As Albert Einstein put it: "Only two things are infinite, the universe and human stupidity—and I'm not sure about the former.")

How could you have been so blind? You must be an idiot. If your spouse isn't saying that to you (and there are a lot of divorce lawyers out there telling me that marriages are on the rocks because mates blame each other for sinking bank accounts or for misplaying the market), then I am sure you are saying it to yourself.

11

Why *didn't* I see the crash coming? Why *didn't* I diversify my holdings? Why *didn't* I realize layoffs were coming? *How* could I have been so dumb? Before you berate yourself too much for misjudging the future—words like nincompoop and brain-dead come to mind—it pays to look at some famous dead-wrong predictions.

Dead Wrong Predictions by the Not-So-Dumb

This "telephone" has too many shortcomings to be seriously considered as a means of communication. The device is inherently of no value to us.
—Western Union internal memo, 1876.

The wireless music box has no imaginable commercial value. Who would pay for a message sent to nobody in particular?
—David Sarnoff's associates in response to his urgings for investment in the radio in the 1920s.

Who the hell wants to hear actors talk?
—H.M. Warner, Warner Brothers, 1927.

I'm just glad it'll be Clark Gable who's falling on his face and not Gary Cooper.
—Gary Cooper, on his decision not to take the leading role in *Gone with the Wind*.

A cookie store is a bad idea. Besides, the market research reports say America likes crispy cookies, not soft and chewy cookies like you make.
—Response to Debbi Fields' idea of starting Mrs. Fields' Cookies.

We don't like their sound, and guitar music is on the way out.
—Decca Recording Co., rejecting the Beatles, 1962.

Heavier-than-air flying machines are impossible.
—Lord Kelvin, president, Royal Society, 1895.

If I had thought about it, I wouldn't have done the experiment. The literature was full of examples that said you can't do this.
>—Spencer Silver, chemist and inventor, on the work that led to the unique adhesives for 3-M's Post-It Notes.

The concept is interesting and well-formed, but in order to earn better than a "C," the idea must be feasible.
>—A Yale University management professor in response to Fred Smith's paper proposing reliable overnight delivery service. (Smith went on to found Federal Express Corp.)

So we went to Atari and said, "Hey, we've got this amazing thing, even built with some of your parts, and what do you think about funding us? Or we'll give it to you. We just want to do it. Pay our salary, we'll come work for you." And they said, "No. So then we went to Hewlett-Packard," and they said, "Hey, we don't need you. You haven't got through college yet."
>—Apple Computer Inc. founder Steve Jobs on attempts to get Atari and Hewlett-Packard interested in his and Steve Wozniak's personal computer.

Professor Goddard does not know the relation between action and reaction and the need to have something better than a vacuum against which to react. He seems to lack the basic knowledge ladled out daily in high schools.
>—1921 *New York Times* editorial about Robert Goddard's revolutionary rocket work.

You want to have consistent and uniform muscle development across all of your muscles? It can't be done. It's just a fact of life. You just have to accept inconsistent muscle development as an unalterable condition of weight training.
>—Response to Arthur Jones, who solved the "unsolvable" problem by inventing Nautilus.

Drill for oil? You mean drill into the ground to try and find oil? You're crazy.
> —Drillers whom Edwin L. Drake tried to enlist in his project to drill for oil in 1859.

Stocks have reached what looks like a permanently high plateau.
> —Irving Fisher, professor of economics, Yale University, 1929.

Airplanes are interesting toys but of no military value.
> —Ferdinand Foch, French military strategist and future commander of the Allied forces in World War I, 1911.

Everything that can be invented has been invented.
> —Charles H. Duell, commissioner, U.S. Office of Patents, 1899.

Louis Pasteur's theory of germs is ridiculous fiction.
> —Pierre Pachet, professor of physiology at University of Toulouse, France, 1872.

The abdomen, the chest, and the brain will forever be shut from the intrusion of the wise and humane surgeon.
> —Sir John Eric Ericksen, British surgeon, appointed Surgeon-Extraordinary to Queen Victoria, 1873.

No flying machine will ever fly from New York to Paris.
> —Orville Wright, circa 1908.

There is no reason anyone would want a computer in their home.
> —President, chairman, and founder of Digital Equipment Corp., 1977.

640K ought to be enough for anybody.
> —Bill Gates, 1981.

There now. Does that make you feel better? People make mistakes. Even extremely intelligent people who should surely know better. No, you're not stupid. As a matter of fact, you're in very good company.

The Stock Market "Geniuses"

My major holding in early 2000 was a stock hovering in the mid-forties. A famous analyst with excellent credentials appeared on CNBC and, in prophetic tones that seemed as assured as the words of Isaiah, predicted that in a few months that stock "must" be selling for $250. Today you can buy it, if you are foolish enough to do so, for less than a penny—*and that's after a one-for-ten reverse stock split.*

To help you get a better picture of what that means, take a look at the three-year chart in Figure 2-1, which shows price (over $400 a share taking the reverse split into account) as well as volume. The only thing I've removed is the name of the company—because frankly I just can't bear the thought of looking at it again. As an ultimate irony, I should probably share with you at this point the fact that I was born in Switzerland. So what's the connection? When it came to investing, I forgot what the Alps look like! See the top of the mountain on the chart? Well when I was a child I knew that mountains reach

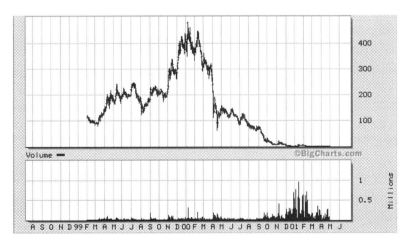

Figure 2-1. The Blech stock: from the womb to the tomb.

peaks and then they go down again. As a supposedly intelligent adult, I "conveniently" ignored this bit of wisdom and managed to incredibly make a molehill out of a mountain, at least as far as my financial holdings were concerned

One of the stars among technology bubble analysts was Henry Blodget of Merrill Lynch. He was responsible for a run-up of Amazon stock after predicting that the company, which still didn't make a profit, would hit $400 a share. As I write this, it's now around $20 (the *New York Financial Journal* has jokingly coined a new word in his honor: *blodget—transitive verb; usually vulgar—to put an enormous price on a stock because your firm is doing the IPO as well as the underwriting for the company*). That prognostication was eclipsed for stupidity by Blodget's repeated recommendations of InfoSpace from its high of $132 all the way down its freefall to a dollar range.

Mary Meeker of Morgan Stanley, the prestigious stock picker who became a media star, was unrestrained in her enthusiasm for priceline.com and drugstore.com among other companies that have now fallen as much as 96 percent in value. As *Business Week* (September 25, 2000) pointed out, Ms. Meeker is typical of the once-obscure Wall Street analysts who joined the glitzy world of celebrity "fortune tellers" during the height of the market frenzy.

The Blodgets and Meekers of this world prove how right Gerald Loeb was when he observed that "In a bull market you don't need analysts, and in a bear market you don't want them." They join the ranks of all the other "brilliant" researchers who blessed us with their "Strong Buy" recommendations for Enron at $90 (now just about a dime), Lucent at $84 (today less than $2), Global Crossing at $60 (you can get it for a penny), WorldCom at $64 (on sale for 28¢), and CMGI at $163 (if you can spare a dollar you can pick up almost four shares today).

In a highly perceptive article by James Surowiecki in *The New Yorker* (March 19, 2001), the author points out: "With few exceptions, analysts didn't see the trouble coming and didn't warn their clients to get out of the way. . . . One exhaustive study which tracked more than 360,000 recommendations over a twelve-year period, found that for the big companies, which together make up most of the stock market's value, analysts' ratings turn out to be predictive of nothing. Darts, anyone?"

Here's the moral you have to take from all this: *If they're getting paid fortunes to predict the turns of the market and can't do better, why beat up on yourself for your own mistakes?*

Why *Can't* the "Experts" Do Better?

An old gypsy proverb says, "There are always two sides to every prediction." Modern "prophets" spend most of their time explaining why their crystal balls were inaccurate. The problem extends far beyond economists and financial analysts. In every field, people are fallible.

In a 1976 essay, the philosophers Samuel Gorovitz and Alastair MacIntyre explored why people make mistakes in spite of the most advanced diagnostic tools and computer assistance. Why would a meteorologist, they asked, find it impossible to predict exactly where a hurricane would take place? They came to the conclusion that there are three possible reasons. The first is ignorance. Maybe science only allows us a limited understanding of how hurricanes behave. A second is ineptitude. Even where scientific knowledge is sufficient to explain and predict, the weatherman, being human, can botch the results. If these were in fact the explanations, then, say Gorovitz and MacIntyre, the problem would be surmountable. The third possible cause, however, isn't. They went so far as to call it "necessary fallibility."[1]

Once we have to move from explaining how things behave to how a *particular* thing will act, we hit a wall that can never be breached. Generally, hurricanes behave in a predictable way. But how Monday's storm will behave on the border between New York and New Jersey is affected by so many uncontrollable, accidental factors that it would require a complete understanding of the entire world and every one of its particulars, which we would call omniscience. And that knowledge belongs only to God, not to people.

Don't Believe Them

If you were to believe everything people tell you, there must have been three million people in the ballpark when Babe Ruth hit his sixtieth homerun. Oh, and there were at least twice as many in attendance when Mark Maguire hit his seventieth homer of the season. At least that's what people would want you to think with regard to every historic moment. "I'm very special. I was there when it happened. See how lucky I am."

People love to boast, even if they have to lie while they're at it.

- Yahoo? He sold it short at $540—exactly when it hit its all-time high.

- Oracle? She bought it at its all-time low and then sold every share when it hit the top.

- Oh no, I was not affected by this downturn, they'll tell you. I even made money by buying puts (that's a strategy that lets you make money when the stock goes *down*) because I knew the market was in for a serious decline.

They're just like all those "lucky people" who assure you that they never *ever* lose money betting at the track.

Please, please, don't believe these arrogant attempts to make you feel small. "Conceit," Bruce Barton, the famous American advertising executive and author, observed, "is God's gift to little men."

Trust me on this: The market doesn't know you by name. It doesn't make a stock go down the day after *you* bought it.

It doesn't wait to go up until after you've sold everything you own. As of this writing, the market lost *almost seven and a half trillion dollars in the past two years.* That almost certainly affected everybody. It doesn't mean that you are stupid; what it does mean is that the market has ups and downs, regardless of your wishes, your personal needs, and the dates of your buy-and-sell orders.

Remember, you're not alone. If you're out of work, realize that the U.S. economy eliminated 185,000 jobs in 2002. They aren't all incompetent. The unemployment rate today stands at almost 7½ percent. That includes professionals and PhDs. For the first time ever, bankruptcy filings last year totaled over 1.5 million for a twelve-month period. These include some very bright people—just like you—who got hammered by an unexpected and unprecedented economic downturn. And if you invested in stocks and now think you look foolish, it's okay to remind yourself that the market is filled with risks. You take them because in the long run stocks have always gone up. The decline of the Dow doesn't brand you a dummy. Take comfort in the knowledge that you're not alone. And, as the Yiddish saying goes, "Everyone can be wise for somebody else—in retrospect."

⌐ The Things You Want to Remember ⌐

■ Making mistakes doesn't make you stupid; it makes you human.

■ The supposed experts of Wall Street who claim to be prophets are far more likely to steer you to "no profit."

■ Fallibility is a fact of life. The only person who never made a mistake in his life is the man your wife keeps reminding you she should have married.

■ Don't believe all the people who try to belittle you (or cover up their own insecurity) by lying about their supposed financial successes. The market didn't single you out for special punishment. Don't be vain enough to think that it knows you by name and tracks your every move.

■ The mantra to repeat after reading this chapter is the insight of William James, the nineteenth-century American psychologist and philosopher: "The art of being wise is the art of knowing what to overlook." Overlook what you did wrong in the past. Move on in the knowledge that momentary defeats are bound to happen because we are not omniscient.

Note

1. Samuel Gorovitz and Alistair MacIntyre, "Toward a Theory of Medical Fallibility," *Journal of Medicine and Philosophy* 1, 51-71 (1976): 63–64.

CHAPTER 3

How Much Are You Worth?

He who dies with the most toys, wins.

—Anonymous slogan
of the eighties

Okay, I reassured you in the last chapter that you're not really stupid. Please let me add, though, one little qualification: You really are an idiot if you bought into the mistaken philosophy that confuses wealth with worth.

Were you one of those who constantly kept calling your broker to find out the latest prices? Did you spend hours before the computer screen checking the movement of your investments? What always amazes me is the reason people give for their hour-by-hour and minute-by-minute need to know. "I have to know how much I'm worth," they explain.

Understand the profound implications of this simple statement: How much I'm worth depends on the fluctuations of market forces over which I have absolutely no control! It's not just the outside world any longer that has come to confuse the value of what people *have* with the value of what they *are*. Far too many of us have internalized this ridiculous notion by defining success in life as the ability to accumulate material possessions. That forces our self-image to constantly waver between success or failure as a human being.

21

"Try not to become a man of success, but rather try to become a man of value." The man who said these words was certainly one of the greatest geniuses in history. His name was Albert Einstein, and this basic truth of life, he added, wasn't relative.

If our worth was really determined by our wealth, we'd have to conclude that the most valuable people in the world today are sports stars, rock artists, entertainment personalities, and CEOs of major corporations. Teachers who guide our children, clergymen who care for our souls, police and firemen who protect our safety, nurses who care for our elderly, servicemen who fight for our country—these, based on their pay scales, are clearly not as vital to American society as a good fielding shortstop who can get a base hit every three or four attempts.

By a remarkable coincidence, two women revered by almost the entire world died in the same week in August 1997. Although they knew each other as friends, their lives couldn't have been more different. One was stunningly beautiful. To maintain herself and her lifestyle, her annual spending was over $1 million. Of that budget, nearly half a million dollars was paid in salaries for a twenty-person staff, including a dresser, a driver, and a secretary. There were annual expenditures of $15,000 on treatments and therapies; $12,000 on exercise, including her personal trainer; $6,400 for her hair, including $459 every two months to highlight her tresses; and $153,000 for her wardrobe. Her friend, for whom even the word "attractive" would have been highly out of place, left an "estate" comprised of the following on her death: Three saris, a pair of sandals, and a book. That's how different were the lives of Princess Diana and Mother Teresa.

The world wept for both of them. For the Princess, it was the tragedy of a Greek epic, the death of an almost divine figure of royalty having her candle extinguished while she still had so much more to live for and accomplish. For Mother Teresa, tears were shed by a world that had been ennobled by the presence of a saint. A heroic figure taught us how high a human being can soar in selfless giving, negation of personal needs to care only about others, and altruism thought attainable only by God, made manifest before our eyes in human form.

Did I mention that among Mother Teresa's final possessions—the saris, the sandals, and the book—there wasn't a single share of stock?! Imagine asking her, "How much are you worth?" Now put your own life into perspective. You are not a better, worthier person if the Dow jumps two hundred points or you get a higher paying job. You are not suddenly a less valuable human being if the Nasdaq tumbles three hundred points or you suddenly get laid off.

Want to know how much you're really worth? Speak to your significant other and remind yourself of the strength of your mutual love. Talk to your children and remind yourself of how they view you as a mother or father. Think about your friends and how much you've added to their lives, and they to yours.

Now take this little quiz and see what you learn from it:

1. Name the five wealthiest people in the world.

2. Name the last five Heisman trophy winners.

3. Name the last five winners of the Miss America contest.

4. Name ten people who have won a Nobel or Pulitzer prize.

5. Name the last half-dozen winners of Academy Awards for best actor and actress.

6. Name the last decade's World Series winners.

How did you do? Okay . . . the point is, none of us remember all the headliners of yesterday. These are no second-rate achievers. They are the best in their fields. But the applause dies. Awards tarnish. Achievements are forgotten. Accolades and certificates are buried with their owners.

Here's another quiz. See how you do on this one:

1. List a few teachers who aided your journey through school.

2. Name three friends who have helped you through a difficult time.

3. Name five people who have taught you something worthwhile.

4. Think of a few people who have made you feel appreciated and special.

5. Think of five people you enjoy spending time with.

6. Name half a dozen heroes whose stories have inspired you.

Easier? The moral: The people who make a difference in your life are not the ones with the most credentials, the most money, or the most awards. They are the ones that care.

Too bad that one of the wealthiest men in the world didn't learn this lesson until it was too late. Sam Walton was the multibillionaire CEO of Wal-Mart, the fourth largest U.S. corporation. As he was lying on his deathbed, he struggled to get out his last three words on earth. He had given his life for his business. In that area, he succeeded beyond anyone's wildest dreams. Yet, it was at a price. He hardly spent any time with his wife, his children, and his grandchildren. He didn't allow himself the moments of loving interaction, of cuddling a grandchild on his lap, of playing and laughing and rejoicing with his loved ones. His final three words? "I blew it!" He had the billions, but by his own admission he had failed.

— What You Want to Remember —

■ What you have is not who you are. Say it over to yourself as many times as you need to until you truly believe it.

- Your portfolio or your salary can't tell you how much you're worth. Only your partners in life can do that— your family, your friends, the people you work with, and the people you love.

- No tombstone ever mentions the amount of money a person leaves behind. Carved in stone, instead, are the qualities of goodness and kindness that continue to live on after our departure from this earth.

- I saved this quote from Ralph Waldo Emerson—the nineteenth-century American Unitarian minister, essayist, poet, and philosopher—for last. That's because I want its insights to linger with you and to help you let go of your preoccupation with your loss of money:

To laugh often and much; to win the respect of intelligent people and the affection of children; to earn the appreciation of honest critics and endure the betrayal of false friends; to appreciate beauty; to find the best in others; to leave the world a little better, whether by a healthy child, a garden patch, or a redeemed social condition; to know even one life has breathed easier because you have lived. This is the meaning of success.

CHAPTER 4

How Expensive Is a Guilt Trip?

My mother always sends me on vacations.
I call them guilt trips.

—Rita Rudner,
comedienne

Hopefully, by now you've gotten past denial. You no longer think you're stupid. You realize what you are is far more important than what you have. Yet, there's still something gnawing at you. You can't really define it. But when you think about it honestly, you realize you're carrying around in your head the heaviest burden on earth. Its name is guilt—and if you allow it, it can destroy you.

We can laugh at the stereotypical Jewish mother who, as Jackie Mason explains, is such an expert at needling her children that she has an honorary degree in "Jewish Acupuncture." It's the Jewish mother who has been immortalized as the woman who gives her son-in-law a present of two ties. When she next meets him and sees him wearing one of them, she gives him a disdainful look and says, "What's the matter? The other one you didn't like?"

Why the "guilt-givers" of the world have become identified with Jewish mothers is something I can't explain. Perhaps because their lives were so precarious, they needed to infuse their children with an extra dose of the psychological feeling of inadequacy that will keep them more firmly attached to their mothers' apron strings. One thing that almost all philosophers and psychologists agree with is that the emotion of guilt has a very important evolutionary basis: We need guilt in order to create an inner conscience that allows us to become civilized. Guilt allows us to feel regret, to be filled with remorse, and to refrain from or repeat wrongs. Without the sense of guilt as it molds the superego, as Sigmund Freud told us, there wouldn't be enough people in the world to serve as policemen to protect society from conscienceless killers.

Why Guilt Is Bad for You

The problem with guilt, though, is that it's both a blessing and a curse. And unfortunately—perhaps even tragically—the moral purveyors of guilt all too often fail to stress its tremendous potential for negative consequences.

Lucy Freeman, in her book, *Guilt: Letting Go*, goes so far as to contend that:

> Guilt in one sense could be called our number one killer. It far surpasses cancer and heart failure, accidents, addictions, suicides and murders, for guilt is a major contributor to all these. Guilt may drive us to suffer physical illness, to commit an accident, to become an addict, to be driven to suicide or murder. If we could rid ourselves of the irrational guilt that is the source of most of our terror and distress, many of us would live longer, and spare ourselves much of the pain of our lives.

Can guilt really be responsible for all that? Even those who won't go as far as Freeman would agree that excessive guilt can have seriously debilitating consequences. That's why I think it's sinful that we don't often enough stress the difference between good guilt and bad guilt.

Good guilt reminds us we're not perfect and challenges us to change. Good guilt is the appropriate response to actions we know are not worthy of us. Good guilt ends up making us happier, finer, and nobler human beings. For example, good guilt is our conscience calling out to us to apologize when we've hurt others and to renew friendships we've allowed to lapse for no reason.

Bad guilt doesn't advise as much as it condemns. It doesn't speak, but it screams. Its major message is to emphasize how unworthy and evil we are, so much so that we can't even believe there is any hope for us to improve ourselves. Bad guilt leads to despair, discouragement, disappointment, and depression. In the simplest sense, bad guilt is crueler than sadism; it turns its masochistic perpetrators into becoming their own victims, with no hope of ever receiving a pardon.

The Antidote to Bad Guilt

One of the major teachings of almost all religions is the beauty of the act of forgiveness. It is a quality we ascribe to God as we seek divine mercy. It is an ideal we aspire to in our personal relationships. We all wrong each other at times, and forgiveness is the healing magic that allows the renewal of friendships and the stability of marriages.

There is only one person to whom we very often choose to deny forgiveness. Unfortunately, that individual is none other than our own self.

Almost everyone knows the Biblical commandment to "love your neighbor as yourself." What most people don't realize is that there are two instructions given here, not one, and in very specific order. The verse is always used to remind us to love others, but we ignore, at our own peril, the first necessary step that has to be taken in order to accomplish the goal of loving others. Love your neighbor, the Bible teaches, *as yourself.*

To be able to fulfill love of neighbor, you first have to be able to love yourself!

It is one of the most profound psychological truths that the deep-seated hatred manifested by tyrants or criminals like Charles Manson is in reality self-hatred turned outward. To be truly human, you must begin with self-acceptance and self-esteem. Only then can you move forward to a feeling of affection for others as well.

The Hassidic Rabbi of Kotsk was right when he witnessed a man beating another and said to his disciples, "See how even while performing an evil act, this Jew is fulfilling the words of the Holy Bible. He is demonstrating that he loves his neighbor as much as he loves himself. We can only pray that he eventually comes to love himself, so that he may alter the way he treats others."

Free at Last

It's time to free yourself from the shackles of bad guilt. It's time to forgive yourself for past sins—both real and imagined. In his book, *How Psychotherapy Works*, Dr. Joe Weiss, a psychotherapist at Mount Zion Research Center in San Francisco, contends that nearly everyone suffers to some degree from a condition diagnosed after the Holocaust by Dr. Robert Lifton, the world-famous psychiatrist, author, and visiting professor of psychiatry at the Harvard Medical School. Lifton calls it "survivor guilt." Survivors of concentration camps felt guilty about surviving. Why them and not their fathers or mothers, their children or siblings? Survivor guilt has been observed in people who lived unscathed through natural disasters, such as earthquakes and floods, when others perished. It was a condition that required therapy for many of the young students at Columbine High School who were not wounded. Guilt, it seems, is such a powerful emotion that it even wants to enter through the back door when there is no reason whatsoever to justify its presence. That's why it's so important not to allow what happens with the stock market, the economy, or your job to rob you not only of your wealth, but of your self-love.

It's okay for you to feel guilty when you forget to buy your spouse a birthday present. After all, you are responsible for a hurtful action. But let me remind you once more, you are not Alan Greenspan. You don't have the power to move markets (and I'm not even so sure about him). You got caught up in a tidal wave that swept you up with millions of others. Could you have sold out at the high? Sure, if you were a prophet. Could you have prevented your company from eliminating your job? Sure, if you were the CEO. Could you have single-handedly turned the economy around? Sure, if you were God. Feeling guilty is to choose depression as a response to loss. Can't you find it in your heart to forgive yourself, even for a crime that you didn't commit?

⌐ What You Want to Remember ⌐

- Guilt has been overplayed as a positive and effective teacher.

- Wisdom requires the ability to differentiate between good guilt and bad guilt. You know it's bad guilt when it doesn't help you improve, but only paralyzes you with despair.

- Loving your neighbor is a noble sentiment. Never forget, though, that according to the way the Bible phrases this famous commandment, loving yourself is a required prerequisite.

- Learn the power of forgiveness even for yourself. Don't remain focused only on your past mistakes. Understand that, as the nineteenth-century Presbyterian minister Henry Ward Beecher said, "I can forgive but I cannot forget," is only another way of saying, "I cannot forgive."

- Remember that the secret of happiness is to be less for "getting" and more forgiving.

CHAPTER 5

Money Isn't Really Your Best Friend

A great fortune is a great slavery.

—Seneca, first-century Roman
statesman and philosopher

Elizabeth Taylor may not be the greatest philosopher of our generation. Yet, some years ago, she responded to an event in her life with an insight from which I believe every one of us could learn a great deal.

Thieves had broken into her safety deposit box. They stole a considerable amount of jewelry. You can only imagine its value when you consider all the men who have lavished precious gifts on her. Reporters asked her after she learned of her loss: "Did you cry?" Her answer was simple: "I don't cry for things that won't cry for me!"

Yes, I remember that at the beginning of this book I told you that you could cry over financial loss. But that doesn't mean that you have to or that you can't eventually find the wisdom to realize that what left you wasn't really your best friend, after all.

In Jewish tradition, there's a saying that during our lifetimes we have three main friends—and when we die, they leave us in exactly the reverse order in which we treated them. No sooner does our soul leave our body, than all of our wealth

31

flees with it as well. Families are more faithful. They walk with us after our passing to the cemetery, our final resting place. Then, they too leave us to go on with their lives. It is only our name, the good deeds we performed for others, and the influence we may have had upon them, that outlive us and offer us a share of immortality.

Strange then, isn't it, that we spend most of our lives chasing after money, spending far less of our time than we should with our families, and spending so little of our efforts to accomplish those things by which we will be remembered! Maybe making a fortune isn't all that it's cracked up to be. Maybe we can even identify with the profound words of the contemporary author Emile Henry Gauvreay: "I was part of that strange race of people aptly described as spending their lives doing things they detest to make money they don't want, to buy things they don't need, to impress people they dislike."

The Problem of Having Too Much

There is a prayer composed by the ancient Greek philosopher, Plato, that we might all recite at the beginning of every day:

> Grant that I may become beautiful in my soul within, and that all my external possessions may be in harmony with my inner self. May I consider the wise to be rich, and may I have such riches as only a person of self-restraint can bear or endure.

The supposed wise saying of our day is, "You can't be too thin or too rich." I've seen all too many examples that prove both these statements are false. "Anorexia" is the medical term for the sickness of people who refuse to acknowledge that too little, in terms of weight, may prove fatal. A good description for the ailment that allows too much wealth to destroy the lives of its owners is the word "affluenza."

Now part of the title of a best-selling book, *Affluenza: The All-Consuming Epidemic*, by John DeGraaf, David Wann, and

Thomas H. Naylor, affluenza is described by the authors as "a painful, contagious, socially-transmitted condition of overload, debt, anxiety and waste resulting from the dogged pursuit of more. It's a powerful virus running rampant in our society, infecting our souls, affecting our wallets and financial well-being, and threatening to destroy not only the environment but also our families and communities." The cure, they inform us, appears to be relegated to the distant future, since "the urge to splurge continues to surge."

Affluenza means knowing how to make money, but not how to live. Affluenza can turn you into an egomaniac. Money can make fools of important persons and it can also make important persons out of fools. Affluenza proves that wealth costs some people everything they are. In the words of twentieth-century philosopher Bertrand Russell, "It is preoccupation with possessions, more than anything else, that prevents men from living freely and nobly."

Let me introduce you to some of the better-known victims of affluenza. I want to take you back to the year 1923, as a group of the world's most successful businessmen met at the Edgewater Beach Hotel in Chicago for a financial planning session. Present were:

The president of the largest independent steel company

The greatest wheat speculator

The president of the New York Stock Exchange

A member of the President's cabinet

The greatest bear on Wall Street

The president of the Bank of International Settlements

The head of the world's greatest monopoly

Individually, these men symbolized what the world so frequently terms "success." Collectively, these men controlled more wealth than there was in the U.S. Treasury. Twenty-five years later, however, their lives told a different story.

> The president of the largest independent steel company (Charles Schwab) had lived on borrowed money the last five years of his life and died penniless.

> The greatest wheat speculator (Arthur Cutten) had died abroad unable to pay his debts.

> The president of the New York Stock Exchange (Richard Whitney) had served a prison term in Sing Sing.

> The member of the President's cabinet (Albert Fall) had been pardoned from prison so he could die at home.

> The greatest bear on Wall Street (Jesse Livermore) had committed suicide.

> The president of the Bank of International Settlements (Leon Fraser) had committed suicide.

> The head of the world's greatest monopoly (Ivar Krueger) had committed suicide.

All of these "successes" spent their lives pursuing money, and not one of them learned how to live!

The Hafts and the Headlines

An excellent, more modern illustration is the story that, for several months in 1998, filled the front pages of *The Washington Post* and *The Wall Street Journal*. I read it as not just the tragic tale of one family destroyed by an excess of wealth, but a modern metaphor for the all-too-common multimillionaires created by the financial bubble of the 1990s.

Herbert Haft grew up in Baltimore, where he lived above his Russian immigrant father's drug store. The family lost the business during the Depression. After World War II, Herbert married and, together with his new wife, Gloria, opened a drug store in Washington. It didn't work out that well, so together they opened another one, a discount drug store, which they called Dart Drug.

Dart Drug grew into a major chain, and along the way the Hafts also acquired ownership of Crown Books, Trak Auto, Shoppers Warehouse, and a net worth estimated to be between $500 million and $1 billion. Their younger son, Ronald, played a peripheral role in the business, but their oldest son, Robert, was a major player. His father paid public tribute to Robert at his fortieth birthday party and spoke movingly about how they had "everything." They enjoyed their mansions in Washington, Florida, California, and Massachusetts.

But by 1998 things had changed. The Hafts weren't spending that much time in their homes. Herbert Haft accused his son, Robert, of trying to take over the business. Gloria Haft sided with Robert. The other son, Ronald, sided with Herbert. Herbert and Gloria's disagreements over money led to the divorce courts. Accusations of sexual and physical abuse, as well as infidelity, became public fodder for gossip by those obsessed with the lives of the "rich and famous." A family that was truly a family for forty-five years was no more. A family that started with husband and wife mortgaging their home, cashing in their babies' savings bonds to open the store where Gloria worked in the front and Herbert ran the pharmacy counter, was no more.

It doesn't have to be that way, you say? Of course it's not inevitable, but it's certainly far more probable to have family discord when there is a fortune of billions of dollars over which to quarrel. Of course *you* would be the exception to the rule. Of course *you* wouldn't be affected at all by having a great deal of money. But even ten centuries ago, the Spanish rabbi and philosopher Bahya Ibn Pakuda wrote that the rule is true for all: "Too much riches are as bad for the soul as too much blood is for the body."

Giving It to Our Children

President George W. Bush, as part of his tax proposal, fought for the repeal of the estate tax. That would mean that the wealthiest Americans would be able to pass on their fortunes to their descendants without a significant portion paid in taxes.

What happened next is almost impossible to believe. In an ad that ran on the Op-Ed page of the February 18, 2001, edition of *The New York Times*, a number of the wealthiest Americans pleaded for maintaining the estate tax even though it would take away considerably from their heirs.

> While we may not be able to ensure that all children start their lives on a level playing field, that is something we should strive for and the estate tax keeps us closer to that ideal.

Those were the words of William Gates. They were seconded by billionaires like Warren Buffett, Steven Rockefeller, George Soros, Ted Turner, and a number of others.

A common thread reiterated by many was the fear that huge inheritances would turn their descendents into idle playboys and parasitic profiteers, benefiting from the arduous work of their ancestors. A goodly number of the wealthiest said that they refused to burden their children with the oppressive consequences of super wealth and that they would rather leave most of their money to charity.

Maybe there's some truth to the comic line that has the successful executive bemoaning what happened to his children and wondering, "How could that be? I gave them everything—everything except poverty."

What God Thinks of Money

If you want to be cynical, then accept the conclusion of English diplomat and author Maurice Baring: "If you would know what the Lord God thinks of money, you have only to look at those to whom he gives it.''

But that isn't really true. Nor did I want the point of this chapter to be a putdown of wealth and another way of saying that love of money is the root of all evil.

In Jewish tradition, God is quoted as teaching Moses the proper role money should play in the lives of people. God showed Moses "a coin of fire." What was the intended symbolism? Fire contains within it two powerfully different potentials. On the one hand, it is a destroyer. Fire burns everything in its way and, left unattended, it can destroy homes, forests, and whatever is in its way. Yet fire is also the key to human creativity. Civilization begins with the ability of humankind to harness its power, to cook, to forge and bend metals. That very duality you see in fire, God explained to Moses, is the same duality implicit in money. With money, God said, "you can build me a sanctuary or fashion a golden calf." With money, we too can become better or bitter people. Wealth is blessing or curse, depending on the use you make of it.

— What You Want to Remember —

- Losing money isn't like losing your best friend. It won't cry for you, and you really shouldn't spend too much time crying for it.

- Money, like everything else, is good in moderation. Be wary of extremes: The green and the overripe fruit cause the worst pain.

- Super wealth brings with it super challenges. Are you sure you're not really better off without millions of dollars for your family to fight over?

- Maybe you lost it because having too much would have taken too much of a toll on you and your family.

- Remember the sage advice of Ralph Waldo Emerson: "Money often costs too much."

Note

1. John DeGraaf, David Wann, and Thomas H. Naylor, *Affluenza: The All-Consuming Epidemic* (San Francisco: Berrett-Koehler, 2001). DeGraaf was the producer of the PBS documentaries "Affluenza" (1996) and "Escape from Affluenza" (1998); David Wann is a former EPA staffer and expert on sustainable lifestyles; and Thomas H. Naylor is professor emeritus in economics at Duke University.

CHAPTER 6

Wealth or Health?

Money isn't everything.
Health is 10 percent.

—Woody Allen, filmmaker,
comedian, and writer

How good are you at remembering radio trivia? Do you know who said the line that caused the longest audience laugh ever recorded? And do you possibly also remember the words that made the audience so hysterical that they couldn't stop laughing for several minutes?

For those too young to have listened to one of the all-time greatest comedians, Jack Benny, I'll tell you the answer. You must know beforehand, though, that Jack Benny's specialty wasn't telling jokes as much as it was playing a specific character. Among many other traits, he adopted the "on-air" personality of a stingy miser. In what was to become the most famous scene of all, a robber accosts Benny and demands, "Your money or your life!" Benny slowly turned his head and looked out at the audience with that classic deadpan expression, saying nothing for just the right length of time. The thief repeats his request, and Benny still remains silent. When prompted once more, "Your money or your life!," Benny says, "I'm thinking, I'm thinking." It brought the house down.

I once met the scriptwriter of that immortal line when I lectured in Los Angeles. He admitted to me that it came about totally by accident. All the scriptwriters in the room were frantically trying to come up with a funny Jack Benny–type response. No one was quite sure how to get the best laugh. When the others in the room pushed this particular script writer for his best line, in desperation he pleaded for more time and said, "I'm thinking, I'm thinking," to which the entire group responded with spontaneous applause, "That's it, that's it."

Now let's do a little thinking about why this line was responsible for such a hysterical response. Jack Benny played "every man," with all of our faults exaggerated. In him, we were able to better be aware of our personal flaws. We know that we all are sometimes a little too stingy. We realize that we often are more concerned with pursuing wealth than maintaining our health.

What the dialogue between the thief and his potential victim pointed out so very clearly is that for many of us the answer to the question, "Your money or your life!," isn't so evident.

Can anyone really be that stingy or stupid? Just look around you and see how many people literally "kill themselves" to make a "living." Now that's surely a paradox that should be evident to all. "Slow down," says the doctor, "or you'll die of a heart attack. It's your money or your life." And the patient's response as he leaves the doctor's office is, "I'm thinking, I'm thinking." And, all too often, widows and orphans can attest to the foolish choice that was made.

What Would *You* Do?

Let's try this imaginary scenario. The stock market never crashed. The economy is in great shape. You've never felt more secure about your job and your future. You have tons of money. During a routine check-up, your doctor discovers you've got a rare and very serious sickness. The good news is that modern medicine has discovered a treatment that will cure you. The bad news is that there is so little of the medicine available that it will cost you almost your entire fortune to procure it.

Unless you are suicidal or the identical twin of the character played by Jack Benny, you will thank God that you are financially able to deal with this problem. You'll spend whatever it takes to make yourself well. After all, money is only a means to an end, not an end in itself. It's only as valuable as what it can do for you. In this case, it can restore you to good health—and that's worth every penny.

Changing the Scenario

Now let's imagine the story somewhat differently. The stock market crashes. You're almost wiped out. But thank God you still have your health. The doctor just told you there's nothing wrong with you. You didn't have to spend your fortune on medical bills, but it disappeared nonetheless.

Now you face the ultimate challenge: Do you allow the loss of your fortune to make you sick as well? Till now you lost money because of market conditions that were totally out of your control. Making yourself sick over what happened, however, is a decision that rests fully in your own hands. How could you willingly make yourself sick over the loss of money if you would have gladly given it all away in order to regain good health?

The Deadly Quartet

For many years, doctors have been warning us to control our weight, our blood pressure, our cholesterol, and our blood sugar levels. This combination of life-threatening factors has been dubbed the "Deadly Quartet" or the "Metabolic Syndrome."

Today, scientific studies confirmed an amazing fact: All four factors in this Deadly Quartet can be dangerously affected by just one key trigger. Believe it or not, it isn't bacteria or viruses that cause the most harm. The major villain is not something that invades us from outside of our bodies; it's the stress we induce in ourselves by the way in which we respond to unpleasant realities.

The ancient practitioners of medicine were not as far removed from modern concepts as we might think. The Greek Stoic philosopher Epictetus, who practiced as a physician into the second century, turns out to have been fairly right when he wrote, "We ought to be more concerned about removing wrong thoughts from the mind than about removing tumors and abscesses from the body."

Here's how contemporary scientists put it: Stress sets off a domino effect in the body's endocrine system. It all starts in a part of the brain called the hypothalamus. Its role is to send a message to the body's master gland, the pituitary. That signals the adrenal glands to release abnormally high amounts of the stress hormone called coritisol. And what does that cause? Abdominal fat storage; elevated insulin levels linked to heart attacks, diabetes, and stroke; high blood sugar and blood pressure; a poor cholesterol profile; as well as other problems.

Yes, all that from stress. Stress caused by the way *you* are mentally dealing with misfortune. I can hardly think of anyone born with more disabilities than Helen Keller. It was she of all people who reminded us that, "God doesn't close one door without opening another. We do the most harm to ourselves if we reflect only upon the door now shut, rather than the one newly opened."

The Marathon "Loser"

Once a year many tens of thousands of people participate in the New York City marathon. Crowds come to cheer for the winner. I want to share with you the story of the "loser"—the person who in 1998 came in dead last, finishing many hours after everyone had completed the race.

Her name is Zoe Koplowitz. She was forty-six years old, and she suffered from a debilitating disease—multiple sclerosis. She'd had it more than twenty years. She could only walk with the aid of two crutches, one slow, painful step at a time.

On a cold day in November, she walked for more than 31 hours and 15 minutes and finished the 26-mile race, limping across the finish line with her left leg dragging. She came in last, but she finished.

Why did she do it? Here was her answer in her award-winning book, *The Winning Spirit, Life Lessons Learned in Last Place*:

> When you are born, God gives you a television set with a hundred channels. Ninety-nine of them have wonderful programs on them. One has only static. Everybody, with no exceptions, has that channel with the static on their set. The only difference is the kind of static you were given on that one channel. And you have a choice. You can sit in front of that one channel for the rest of your life and look at the static or you can get up and change the channel. My commitment in life is to change the channel as frequently as possible.

So what's your static? You lost your money? Stop obsessing and CHANGE THE CHANNEL. If you still have your health, you're a very lucky person. And if you allow your health to be ruined because of lost money, you're no better than Jack Benny who had to think about whether his money or his life was more important.

⌐ What You Want to Remember ⌐

- Between health and wealth, the one with the "h" brings happiness; the one with the "w" brings worry.

- "Your money or your life!" is an easy question to answer. Unfortunately, all too many of us give the wrong response.

- Worry and stress are subtle forms of self-destruction.

- The stock market doesn't stay up nights worrying about you. Why should you treat it better than it treats you?

- Instead of worrying about what's wrong and making yourself sick, change the channel you're tuning into and watch all the other good programs.

- Remember the advice of English author and Anglican prelate William Ralph Inge: "Worry is interest paid on trouble before it falls due." Don't allow stress to take over your life. Monetary losses are recoverable, but destroying your health can cost you your life.

CHAPTER 7

What Would You Do with It?

If a man is proud of his wealth,
he should not be praised until
it is known how he employs it.

—Socrates, fifth-century B.C.
Athenian philosopher

You're depressed because you lost a fortune. Doesn't it make sense for you to stop and think about what you would do if the money was all still there—and more? You realize that those little green pieces of paper are merely a means to an end, not an end in and of themselves. So what is it that you can't do now that you would have done before?

Losing a lot of money, just like suddenly making millions, forces you to confront your real priorities in life. To help you to understand yourself—your real needs, desires, and values—truthfully answer this telling question: What do you believe is missing in your life that having a great deal of money would supply?

Listen to this story and see if it relates at all to you.

45

The Mexican Fisherman

An American investment banker was at the pier of a small coastal Mexican village when a small boat with just one fisherman docked. Inside the small boat were several large yellow-finned tuna. The banker complimented the Mexican on the quality of his fish and asked how long it took to catch them. The Mexican replied: "Only a little while." The banker then asked why he didn't stay out longer and catch more fish. The Mexican said he had enough to support his family's immediate needs.

The banker was puzzled and then asked, "But what do you do with the rest of your time?" The Mexican fisherman said, "I sleep late, swim a little, play with my children, take a *siesta* with my wife Maria, stroll into the village each evening where I sip wine and play guitar with my *amigos*. I have a full and busy life, *Señor*."

The banker scoffed, "I am a Harvard MBA and could help you. You should spend more time fishing and with the proceeds buy a bigger boat. With the proceeds from the bigger boat you could buy several boats. Eventually, you'll have a fleet of fishing boats. Instead of selling your catch to a middle man, you would sell directly to the processor, eventually opening your own cannery. You would control the product, processing, and distribution. You would need to leave this small coastal fishing village and move to Mexico City, then Los Angeles, and eventually to New York City where you will run your expanding enterprise."

The fisherman asked, "But, *Señor*, how long will this all take?" To which the banker replied, "Five to ten years."

"But what then, *Señor*?" The banker laughed and said, "That's the best part. When the time is right, you would announce an IPO and sell your company's stock to the public and become very rich. You would be worth millions!"

"Millions, *Señor*? Then what?" The banker said, "Then you would retire, move to a small coastal fishing village, take *siestas* with your wife, play with your kids, and stroll to the village in the evenings where you would sip wine and play your guitar with your *amigos*."

How remarkable. The very things that the fisherman could look forward to at the end of a long and arduous process that would require him to put his life on hold are those all-important parts of life he already enjoys in his semi-poverty.

What would having more do for him? Prevent him from presently enjoying family and friends, laughing and living, being independent and free of the worries associated with major financial investments. And of course we all realize that the five to ten years that the banker estimated would be needed will stretch out far longer as greed for more as well as unexpected difficulties turn the project into a lifelong journey. How much smarter to remember the advice of the first-century Roman philosopher, Juvenal: "It is sheer madness to live in want in order to be wealthy when you die."

Who Wants to Be a Millionaire?

Regis Philbin took America by storm a few years ago when he turned the program *Who Wants to Be a Millionaire* into the most popular show on television. As several critics have pointed out, the producers of the show didn't even put a question mark at the end of the title. After all, what they imply is that it isn't even a question. Everyone wants to get rich.

Well, here's a surprise for you. In an exclusive AARP *Mod-*

ern Maturity survey, "Money and the American Family," 27 percent of men and a startling 40 percent of women said "no" when asked whether they would like to become wealthy. More than half defined wealthy as acquiring $500,000 or less in total assets. In fact, only 8 percent said it would take $1 million to make them feel wealthy.[1]

How can we explain why so many people have an aversion to getting rich? Four out of five of those surveyed said they feared that wealth would turn them into greedy people who consider themselves superior. Three-fourths of the respondents said that wealth promotes insensitivity. Even those who say they would like to be wealthy share that negative view of how the rich behave.

To their credit, most Americans are smart enough to realize that money can't buy such intangibles as self-esteem, family togetherness, happiness, or love. Even if they had all the wealth in the world, they realize that what really matters in life isn't based on financial status. In response to the crucial question, "Can money buy peace of mind?," 52 percent of Americans said "no." That means the majority of people realize that having money won't be the answer to all of their problems. In fact, many have come to the opposite conclusion: A sudden fortune can be a curse instead of a blessing.

"Help Me, Doctor, I'm Rich"

Dennis Pearne is a clinical psychologist and a pioneer in the emerging field of wealth counseling. His specialty is treating clients with "sudden wealth syndrome." Those are people who inherited large sums of money, won the lottery, or sold their Internet businesses for billions of dollars.

Now they were faced with the dilemma of, "What do I do next?" How many cars can you buy? How many homes can you own? As the Yiddish saying goes, even the wealthiest man can't eat more than one dinner.

According to Pearne:

Sudden wealth creates issues that go way beyond money. The money can cause traumatic responses and lead to shame, anger, confusion, isolation and guilt, among other things. With inherited money, you hear stories of what goes on in families—the control game, blackmail, gender discrimination, resentment children have at being raised by nannies, and a whole host of psychological issues.

The way Pearne has helped people the most is by working with them on a value-based exploration in order to focus on proper priorities. Together, the "wealth counselor" and the "sudden wealth victim" explore basic questions of life: What is the relative importance of living a wealthy lifestyle versus accumulating more wealth versus helping friends and family versus philanthropy? What do you do with the money you will never need for yourself? How would you want the world to improve—and what can you do now personally to turn your ideal into reality?

One of the most striking things Pearne has found is that when his clients seriously reconsider their options in life, they invariably choose to devote themselves to social change.

"Money is a neutral object, a tool that can be used positively or negatively," he said. "The power of receiving a lot of money is so great it can destroy someone's life or empower someone to have a much better life. It all depends on how you deal with it."

The Lottery Winners

Colin Sampson thought he was a very lucky man. A former plasterer, he was the much-surprised winner of 5.4 million pounds in Britain's national lottery in 1997. A little less than a year later, this same stressed-out lottery millionaire told magistrates that the pressure of wealth and fame had driven him to a specialized form of gardening therapy—growing marijuana.

"Maybe this is a lesson for all lottery winners," defending

solicitor George Tierney told the bench. "My client says that from the point of the win onwards, his life has been absolute hell. He can't do anything at all without attracting attention."

Mr. Sampson detailed the effect of the "curse of the lottery" on his previously uneventful life. After an initial spending spree, including days of clothes buying and paying for a holiday for twenty-five relatives in Jamaica, the bad times began. The family's children were pursued at school and outside their new luxury home. He and his wife had considerable difficulties adjusting and she could not deal with the media attention. Rather than going to the doctor and pleading for some kind of drug assistance, the defense attorney pleaded that Mr. Sampson turned to marijuana as a last resort to help him get over what he calls "the curse of the win."

But that doesn't mean winning the lottery has to have a sad ending. Consider the story of Eleanor Boyer, a retired buyer of chemicals and office supplies for American Cyanamid, who won the New Jersey lottery in 1988, earning a lump sum of $11.8 million. What did she do with her newfound wealth? The 72-year-old woman planned to give it all away, about half to the church in which she worshipped all her life, and the rest to the town rescue squad, the volunteer fire department, and some of the other groups that serve the town she grew up in.

"No new car, no vacation," she told *The New York Times*. "My life is no different. I have given it up to God. I live in His presence and do His will, and I did that from the start." Ron Czajkowski, vice president of the New Jersey Hospital Association, said, "The idea of somebody turning over all of that sum of money to the community and to the church is inspiring. It kind of makes you step back and think about what our priorities are."

So What Would *You* Do?

There's no better way to understand people, psychologists say, than to see how they spend their money. "Show me your checkbook stubs," said the noted psychologist, Erich Fromm, "and I'll tell you everything about yourself." Self-indulgence or selflessness? Wine, women, and song or charitable works? Hedonism or helping others? Forsaking God because you no longer need Him or feeling more spiritually connected out of gratitude for your good fortune?

I know we all claim we would have the right priorities. But what did you do with your money when you had it? Is it possible that it's gone because God wants you to rethink what's really important and how you will handle wealth if God chooses to bless you with it once more? Answer yourself honestly, and you may discover that losing it the first time was a blessing. Getting another chance, some day in the future, will make you not only rich but also fulfilled and blessed.

⌐ What You Want to Remember ⌐

- Don't waste your life pursuing money that will allow you to be happy "some day in the future." Think of those things you plan to do once you are wealthy, and see how many of them are possible to be enjoyed right now.

- Not everyone wants to be a millionaire. Some people are smarter. As nineteenth-century British critic and thinker John Ruskin put it: "It is physically impossible for a well-educated, intellectual, or brave man to make money the chief object of his thoughts."

- Sudden wealth brings with it many problems, chief among them being establishing personal priorities.

- How you spend your money speaks volumes about your values. That's why winning the lottery can prove to be either a curse or a blessing.

- "What would you do with it?" is not just a financial question, but a spiritual one as well. Perhaps we need to know the right answers before God will give us the opportunity to carry out our wishes.

Note
1. *Modern Maturity*, May 1, 2001.

CHAPTER 8

"Thou Shalt Not Covet"

Every time a friend succeeds,
I die a little.

—Gore Vidal

For Jews and Christians alike, the Decalogue—the Ten Commandments—summarize the most important teachings of the entire Bible. The Bible tells us that these commandments were given on two tablets, five laws on one and five on the other. The reason? They deal with two different categories of religious concern. The first five teach us about our responsibilities to God. The last five summarize our obligations with respect to our fellow human beings.

The latter begin with three warnings that encompass very serious sins: You shall not murder, you shall not commit adultery, you shall not steal. Following these, expressing yet a higher level of moral responsibility, the law that comes next teaches that we can even be guilty for sinful speech: "You shall not bear false witness against your neighbor."

It is the last Commandment, though, that commentators explain is meant to bring us to the highest level of holiness. It demands not only that we control our actions and our speech, but even our thoughts. It addresses a universal human failing

53

and obviously believes that we can overcome it: "You shall not covet your neighbor's house; you shall not covet your neighbor's wife, nor his manservant, nor his maidservant, nor his ox, nor his donkey, nor anything that is your neighbor's."

These five major laws of interpersonal relationships follow an obvious and logical sequence. They're clearly listed in ascending order of difficulty. Not to murder? Pretty easy. Adultery? Well, I'll have to try hard. Not to steal *anything,* even some paper clips at the office? Very difficult. I can't even share some juicy gossip just because it may not be totally true? You've got to be kidding. And you want me not to covet my neighbor's house or his car? Now *that's* really stretching it, isn't it? These laws, just like physical exercise, move to ever more complicated levels. That's a good reason why they follow one after the other.

But scholars suggest another way of looking at the sequence of these commandments. Appearing on the second tablet, laws six through ten can be understood as teaching a profound idea if we study them in *reverse* order, from bottom to top.

To make it clearer, let's list Commandments six through ten:

1. You shall not murder.

2. You shall not commit adultery.

3. You shall not steal.

4. You shall not bear false witness against your neighbor.

5. You shall not covet. . . .

Looking at them from bottom up, what the Bible is teaching us in a very insightful way is how to understand the root cause of evil. How is it possible for someone to murder a fellow human being? How is it possible to justify unfaithfulness to oneself and to sleep with another's mate? Well, the sequence of the Commandments tells us how to get to the *bottom* of these seemingly incomprehensible actions. Just like the foundation of a house is at the bottom, so too is the cause of crimes against others in the list of the Ten Commandments. The root of a tree is responsible for everything that goes on above it. So, too, the "root cause" of all major sins is coveting. You tell yourself that you deserve it more than your neighbor. Envy motivates you to try to get what you want by bearing false witness in court. If that doesn't work, you allow yourself to steal. If the object of your desire is your neighbor's wife, your coveting leads to adultery. And if none of these prove possible, then the only solution for your insatiable lust is to murder.

That's why coveting concludes the Decalogue. It is both the end as well as the beginning. It is the most demanding Commandment, and it concludes the list of all others because it is the key to their violation, the "foundation" of motive that can even lead to murder.

Keeping Up with the Joneses

To understand why the Dow Jones is so important to us, we have to realize its relationship to the American ideal of "keeping up with the Joneses." Our obsession for acquiring wealth has far less to do with our personal wants than with our refusal to have less than others. We have to face up to the truth that, as the movie producer Frank Ross put it, "It is not so much what we haven't, but what others have that makes for unhappiness."

That's why there is a multibillion-dollar industry in the world today whose purpose is the systematic propagation of envy, the acceptance of the new tenth commandment, which now reads, "You *shall* covet." The name of the industry is advertising. Its goal, as frankly admitted by B. Earl Puckett, president of Allied Stores Corporation, is this: "It is our job to make men and women unhappy with what they have."

"I Have to Have It–or I'll Die"

Every few months, fashions change. What is "in" one month is "out" the next. One week you're an outcast if you're not wearing a certain kind of sneakers. The next week, you're out of date and a geek if you haven't switched to another brand. Why must you constantly have something else? Because big business needs consumers. So consumers have to be taught what they need rather than to have their real needs met.

There's no big secret which emotion Madison Avenue wants to appeal to most. Gucci was brave enough to admit it when it called a new perfume it was trying to popularize, "Envy." Remarkable, isn't it, that what the Bible, the Greeks, the early Buddhists, the followers of almost all major religions, have identified as the basic cause of human suffering—the sin of envy—has become the very feeling the age of advertising wants us to strongly embrace.

In his groundbreaking work, *Ways of Seeing*, British author and social critic Joshua Berger concludes that envy is the underlying basis of all advertisements and the deadliest of the Seven Deadly Sins, the only one that lacks a positive side and is evil in and of itself.

How many times a day are we told not to be happy with what we have because others have more? Thomas Clapp Patton, in his book *Envy Politics*, gives us the staggering figure that Americans are exposed to about 3,000 ads a day. Big-city newspapers consist of 70 to 90 percent ads rather than news. The subliminal message is always the same: Whether you really need it or not, don't be without what other people have.

That's the real meaning of the common expression often heard from shopping fanatics. "If I don't get it, I'll die." How can the word "die" be applied to the lack of a material object? Only because if someone else can afford it and I can't, that makes me a "nothing." And a "nothing" is as good as dead.

How Much Is Enough?

If the desire for something is based on need, then fulfillment brings contentment. If the goal, however, is to overcome the need to covet the acquisitions of others, then we are doomed to disappointment and to ever-greater dissatisfaction. There's always somebody who has a little bit more—enough at least to stir up within us sufficient envy to prevent us from being content with what is ours.

The New York Times carried an interview with a man named Nelson Peltz. Investing in troubled companies in the 1980s, he appeared on the *Forbes* list of the richest executives for almost a decade. His net worth is now estimated at $890 million. But listen to what he says in the interview: "I'm like old money these days. See these young guys worth three billion to four billion and you think to yourself, what have I done wrong?"

Never mind that Nelson Peltz will never be able to spend all of the money he has. There are people ahead of him in the race for wealth, so envy makes him a loser in his own mind.

Envy Addiction

If you need any more powerful proof that coveting irrationally controls people, consider the countless cases of individuals addicted to the Home Shopping Network or to eBay. They readily admit they can't control themselves to keep from buying things they don't need and don't have the money for. These are people who no longer have space in their home to store all of what they buy. They don't even have the time to open the boxes or unwrap them. They have to rent storage lockers for their purchases. Yet they continue buying and buying. What is involved in their own minds is their mistaken definition of self-worth. It's as if our subconscious is telling us, "Damn the cost. Let other people know I'm as good as they are."

"Envy addicts" got some great news from Federal Judge Matthew F. Kennelly in Chicago: The law forgives what is today considered an understandable obsession. As reported in *The New York Times* of May 25, 2001:

Elizabeth Randolph Roach could not stop shopping, her lawyer told a judge. She shopped for things she did not need, things she did not want, designer clothes and jewelry she never even wore. A shopping addiction, her lawyer said, compelled Ms. Roach to buy a $7,000 belt buckle at Neiman Marcus, amass seventy pairs of shoes at one time, and become so enthralled with shopping in London that she racked up a $30,000 bill and missed her plane back home. (Remember the great Henny Youngman line that he didn't report the theft of his credit card because "the thief was spending less with it than his wife"?) And it was the shopping, argued her lawyer, Jeffrey Steinback, that propelled her to steal nearly a quarter of a million dollars from the consulting company she worked for by padding her expense accounts.

Judge Kennelly *agreed* and spared Ms. Roach from going to prison, reducing what could have been an eighteen-month jail sentence because he said she was using her shopping addiction to "self-medicate" her chronic depression.

"Envy addicts" make sure to pass on their sickness to the next generation. From *The Wall Street Journal*, a huge headline blares forth the news that "Italian Firm Fashions a Look Tailor-Made for Indulgent Parents." The ad proceeds to tell us that a company named Pinco sells a line of children's clothes that's catching on like wildfire in America. Dresses for six-year-olds costing over $600 with $200 handbags to match hardly stay on the racks for a full day. Pinco makes clear who their target audience is: "For mothers who regard their children as fashion accessories." No, they're not just kids with their own identities. They're reflections of our status, our worth, and how much we can afford to be like the people whose lives we covet.

We've created a climate where an anonymous author on the Internet wrote that if King David were writing his Twenty-third Psalm today, it would more probably read like this:

The Lord is my shepherd, I shall not want
He leadeth me to Neiman Marcus
He giveth me energy for shopping
He restoreth my checkbook
He teacheth me to make restaurant reservations
He leadeth me past K-Mart for mine own sake
Yea, though I walk by Target
I shall not go in, for Thou art with me
Thy fashionable clothes, they comfort me
Thou preparest diamond jewelry for me in the presence of
mine enemies
Thou anointest my face with Chanel cosmetics
My cup overflows
Surely designer clothes shall follow me to the end of my days
And I will walk on Rodeo Drive forever
Amen

The Poor Professor

He is a dear friend of mine. To maintain his privacy, I'll call him Harry. As a college professor who recently received tenure, he makes an adequate salary, his articles have been published in a number of prestigious journals, and his life is intellectually rewarding and stimulating. He has a happy marriage, three wonderful children, and a very suitable middle-class home.

It is now twenty years after his high school graduation and he is invited to a class reunion. He decides to attend and to find out what happened to his old classmates. As he meets his old friends, he finds that he is not the most successful of his class. Some have more money than he does, even though he knows he was brighter than they were. Others have wives who seem to be more sophisticated and more beautiful than his. When they talk about their children, some are the parents of youngsters with more accomplishments than his. As he leaves, he notices how many others have better, more expensive cars.

He returns home that evening with a gnawing feeling of pain inside of him that he cannot really explain. He was so happy with his life when he left the house to go to the reunion. Now he is consumed with envy. He is dissatisfied with his job, his home, his wife, his life. And what has really changed? Not one single aspect of his reality! But he is no longer content because he has violated the Tenth Commandment. Coveting is not a sin that brings punishment from God. It is a sickness of the soul that brings with it automatic consequences of pain, bitterness, and frustration.

What Are You Really Most Upset About?

Now it's time to ask yourself the question that is the point of this chapter. You lost a lot of money. You lost your job. Your retirement fund went from a 401(k) to a 201(k). Are you really grieving about what you no longer have or what other people still do? Is it because you don't have enough for your need or for your greed? If there were no one else to whom to compare yourself, would you still feel so depressed? How much of what you're feeling isn't the result of enormous financial decline as much as uncontrollable envy of other people who escaped the effects of the stock market crash?

Some people aren't happy, goes a famous Yiddish proverb, unless others suffer from greater misfortunes. Be honest with yourself as to what's really troubling you. If your prime problem is envy, heed the advice of Claudian, the fourth-century Roman poet: "He who covets is always poor."

⏤ What You Want to Remember ⏤

- Coveting is not only a sin but also a crime that consumes its keeper.

- To envy what others have is to ensure that you will never find contentment.

■ Even as the Bible counsels, "You shall not covet," contemporary society is controlled by the advertising media whose creed is to make us dissatisfied with what we have and to make us covet what we don't need.

■ Envy can never find satisfaction. There will always be those who have more than we do.

■ Envy causes us to act irrationally. A great part of the healing process for the financially battered depends upon our ability to give up comparing and coveting, and replacing those acts with contentment and thanksgiving for our own blessings.

CHAPTER 9

What You Have Left

Reflect upon your present blessing,
of which every man has many;
not on your past misfortunes,
of which all men have some.

—Charles Dickens

Here's a strange quirk about human nature: "We seldom think of what we have, but always of what we lack," said Arthur Schopenhauer, the nineteenth-century German philosopher.

You're poor, you think to yourself; your career is over; you're sure you're a miserable failure; and so you fall into depression. You remember what you had just a year ago and you're despondent because of how much you've lost in such a short time. What's remarkable is that the man who had a $100 million and is now down to his last $10 million is just as distraught, if not more so, than the person who had $1 million and is down to $100,000. I once read a satirical observation that the person with $10 million is no happier than the person with $9 million. So all right, maybe the numbers are different for you in this economy. But when you're downcast about all the dollars you no longer have, doesn't it make sense to stop and consider all your blessings that still remain?

Hunger and Poverty

Maybe it never meant much to you when your mother tried to get you to finish your meal by telling you how many destitute children in other countries would be grateful for it. "So let *them* eat it," you felt like responding. Other people's problems, you always felt, weren't your concern.

But now that you're cursing your fate and considering yourself cruelly deprived because you've suffered a serious financial setback, it might be worthwhile to remind yourself of your place in this world:

- Throughout history, famine has struck at least one area of the world every few years.

- Most of the developing countries of Africa, Asia, and Latin America have barely enough food for their people.

- Approximately half a billion people throughout the world are seriously malnourished.

- According to the World Bank's annual "World Development Indicators" report, about 1.2 billion people live on less than one dollar a day. That number has remained approximately constant since 1987.

- About 57 percent of the world's population in the sixty-three poorest countries live on less than an average of two dollars a day.

- One-sixth of the world's population, mainly in Europe, North America, and Japan, enjoy nearly 80 percent of the world's income and live on an average of seventy dollars a day.

So, even now, how are you really doing? After you've deducted all your losses, do you still believe you're entitled to bewail your fate? There's no better advice than that given almost two thousand years ago by Marcus Aurelius, the Roman

Emperor and philosopher: "Of the things you have, select the best and then reflect how eagerly you would have sought them if you did not have them."

Looking Around You

Whenever you're feeling down about money, I suggest you read the following poem written by Maurice McGhea:

The World Is Mine[1]

Today, upon a bus, I saw a lovely girl with golden hair.
I envied her, she seemed so gay, and wished I were as fair.
When suddenly she rose to leave,
I saw her hobble down the aisle,
O God, forgive me when I whine.
I have two legs. The world is mine.
And then I stopped to buy some sweets.
The lad who sold them had such charm.
I talked to him—he seemed so gay—
If I were late, 'twould do no harm.
And as I left he said to me: "I thank you.
You have been so kind.
It's nice to talk with folks like you.
You see," he said, "I'm blind."
O God, forgive me when I whine.
I have two eyes. The world is mine.
Later, walking down the street, I saw a child with eyes of blue.
He stood and watched the others play; it seemed he knew not what to do.
I stopped a moment, then I said: "Why don't you join the others, dear?"
He looked ahead without a word, and then I knew he couldn't hear.

O God, forgive me when I whine.
I'm blessed indeed. The world is mine!

Whenever I read these words—and I reread them often—
I'm ashamed of myself for pitying my financial portion in life!

The $160,000 Blessing

One more thing. Do you have any children? I just read an
amazing statistic: The government recently calculated the cost
of raising a child from birth to age eighteen and came up with
$160,140 for a middle-income family. Talk about sticker
shock! You might think the best course of action would be not
to have children if you want to be "rich." The very opposite is
true.

In a moving sermon that has been much quoted, Pastor
Jim Hayford, Sr., of the Eastside Foursquare Church in Bo-
thell, Washington, put this statistic into perspective:

Actually $160,000 plus isn't so bad when you break it down.
It translates into $8,897 a year, $741 a month, $171 a week,
a mere $24 per day, just a dollar an hour! One might ask the
question; "What do you actually get for $160,140?"
Naming rights. First, middle and last!
Glimpses of God every day.
Giggles under the covers every night.
More love than your heart can hold.
Butterfly kisses and Velcro hugs.
Endless wonder over rocks, ants, clouds, and warm cookies.
A hand to hold, usually covered with jam.
A partner for blowing bubbles, flying kites, building sand
castles, and skipping down the sidewalk in the pouring rain.
Someone to laugh yourself silly with no matter what the boss
said or how your stocks performed that day [emphasis mine].

For $160,140, you never have to grow up.

You get to finger-paint, carve pumpkins, play hide-and-seek, and never stop believing in Santa Claus.

You have an excuse to keep reading the Adventures of Piglet and Pooh, *watching Saturday morning cartoons, going to Disney movies, and wishing on stars.*

You get to frame rainbows, hearts, and flowers under refrigerator magnets and collect spray painted noodle wreaths, hand prints set in clay for Mother's Day, and cards with backward letters for Father's Day.

For $160,140, there is no greater bang for your buck.

You get to be a hero just for retrieving a Frisbee off the garage roof, taking the training wheels off the bike, removing a splinter, filling the wading pool, coaxing a wad of gum out of bangs, and coaching a baseball team that never wins but always gets treated to ice cream regardless.

You get a front row seat to history to witness the first step, first word, first bra, first date, and first time behind the wheel. You get to be immortal.

You get another branch added to your family tree, and if you're lucky, a long list of limbs in your obituary called grandchildren.

You get an education in psychology, nursing, criminal justice, communications, and human sexuality that no college can match.

In the eyes of a child, you rank right up there with God. You have all the power to heal a boo-boo, scare away the monsters under the bed, patch a broken heart, police a slumber party, ground them forever, and love them without limits, so one day they will, like you, love without counting the cost.

That's where Pastor Hayford's sermon ends. In our family, my grandmother summed it up best, when, pointing to her children, she would proudly say, "I am a multimillionaire. Just look at them."

Better Than Winning the Kentucky Derby

There are things our children give us that we often lose sight of. In reality, they mean more than everything in the world. I was reminded of it by six words said at the Belmont Stakes horse race in June 1998, the third leg of the Triple Crown. It was a thrilling race, literally a photo finish with Victory Gallup beating Real Quiet by a nose.

The owner of the horse that lost was a man named Mike Pegran. His horse, Real Quiet, had already won the Kentucky Derby and the Preakness and now, keeping up this pace, it could have become the first Triple Crown winner in many years. In replays of the race that night you could see the excitement on Pegran's face every time the camera came his way. Then, in the very last millisecond of the race, his horse lost. That meant not going down in the history books as the owner of a Triple Crown winner. That meant not winning the half-million-dollar prize for this race and not winning the $5-million bonus that VISA had offered for winning all three races. The camera caught the look of bewilderment and shock and then deep sorrow on Mike Pegran's face. Everything he had worked for, waited for, spent for, hoped for, for so many months, had come to nothing in a fraction of a second. You could see the heartache in his body language.

He was holding his five-year-old daughter, Samantha, in his arms all during the race, lifting her up so that she could watch the race. When the race ended there was a reporter standing nearby as Samantha put her arms around her dejected father and said to him these six words: "But Daddy, you still have me."

I hope that Mike Pegran never forgets those words that his daughter said to him. And I hope during those days when things go badly for us—and there will surely be such days—that we will also not forget what she said. When we lose a prize or a cash bonus or a job that we really wanted to have or the tennis game that we really felt we should have won or something else that hurts to lose, we need to remember what really counts most in life and what doesn't. If Mike Pegran has a daughter *that* loving and smart, he's already won the Triple Crown of life, no matter where his horse finished—provided he appreciates his blessing.

And How Much Are Grandchildren Worth?

Life often forces us to make important choices. Our decisions reflect our values, our priorities, and our attitudes to money and prestige. Let me tell you about a very special woman, a Jewish judge who was offered the position of Associate Justice of the Supreme Court of the United States—and her name is not Ruth Bader Ginsburg.

You might never have heard of Ruth Bader Ginsburg if Judith Smith Kaye had accepted that position. But she turned it down as she had also turned down the opportunity of serving as Attorney General, with Janet Reno taking her place. Judith Smith Kaye is the Chief Judge of the State of New York. She is so highly respected that at the recent annual meeting of the American Bar Association, she was asked to speak ten times. Initially, when she met with President Clinton and he offered her the position of Attorney General, she turned it down because she said she preferred being a judge. She was then offered the position of Chief Judge of the State of New York, which she accepted. But four days before she was to be sworn in, Justice Byron White announced that he would leave the U.S. Supreme Court, and Judge Kaye was placed on top of the list of candidates to replace him. She asked that her name not be considered. Why? To be considered for one job, she said, right after she had accepted another, would exhibit a lack of character and loyalty to principle. Besides, she added, staying in New York, I can continue to visit my granddaughter.

You see, Judith Smith Kaye, Chief Judge of the State of New York, stops by to see her granddaughter every single day on her way to her Manhattan courtroom. That's love of family. During the convention of the American Bar Association she was very busy, not only speaking ten times, but also hosting a dinner in her home for some of the leaders of that organization and their spouses. What did she serve for dinner? *The New York Times* said she went to Zabar's and bought smoked salmon, cream cheese, bagels, and knishes. *The New York Times* article about her concluded with this paragraph: "By Tuesday the Bar convention was winding down and Judge Kaye could return to her normal routine, including her first visit in nearly a week with her granddaughter. While thirteen thousand lawyers were meeting and talking, nine-month-old Sonia had sprouted a new tooth. In the scheme of things, Judge Kaye was asked, which event mattered more. She replied: 'It's not even close.'"

So if you're counting your millions, don't forget to include your grandchildren. Gore Vidal was surely unrealistic when he advised, "Never have children, only grandchildren." But he certainly captured the truth about the very special relationship grandparents have with their grandchildren. How much is that worth? There isn't enough money in the world to buy it.

"All You Need Is Love"

And, of course, the Beatles were right: "All you need is love, love is all you need."

If you love someone and someone loves you, you've got to be grateful—because you are among the most blessed people on earth. Don't look at your own bank account; check out your love account. Make daily deposits with endearing words to your loved one. You'll discover that this is the only bank in the world that will permit you to make greater withdrawals than you deposited.

Let me tell you a love story. It is not the usual kind of a love story, not the Hollywood kind, but I think it is a love story just the same. Francine Klagsbrun ends her book, *Married People: Staying Together in the Age of Divorce,* with this story: After having interviewed hundreds of couples, after having read all the books of all the experts on the subject of marriage, after having studied all the charts and graphs and statistics, she goes home for Rosh Hashanah, the Jewish New Year, to be with her parents, as she does every year. And she grumbles as she does it. She and her husband would rather be with their own friends, in their own synagogue. But she figures: Her father is eighty-five, her mother is eighty-four—how many more years do they have left? So she goes. And this is the way she describes what she sees in her parents' home. This is the last page of the book:

> My father has spent most of the afternoon dressing, a slow process for him. He is ready to leave for synagogue now, to pray for the New Year. My mother will go with him tomorrow, but tonight she is putting last minute touches on the holiday meal. He walks over to her for final inspection. She fixes his tie.
>
> "Remember," she says, "if you get tired walking, stop and rest. You don't have to be the first in the synagogue."
>
> "But I don't have to be the last either," he answers, teasing about her constant worries.
>
> She brushes a piece of dust from his shoulder. He leans down and kisses her on her lips.
>
> "Happy New Year," he says softly.
>
> "Happy New Year," she answers. She looks at him for a second, then kisses him back. "And next year again."[2]

Do you think it mattered to either one of them what their portfolio was worth? They had something far more precious. Maybe it takes their number of years to appreciate it, but all of us can surely learn from them that if you survive to old age with a caring and loving partner, you are more successful than the richest person in the world.

Let the Bard Have the Last Word

Who could have described love better than William Shakespeare? Let his moving words close this chapter and remind us always that if you have love, you still have far more than you ever lost:

Sonnet 116

Let me not to the marriage of true minds

Admit impediments: love is not love

Which alters when it alteration finds,

Or bends with the remover to remove.

Oh no! It is an ever-fixed mark,

That looks on tempests and is never shaken;

It is the star to every wandering bark,

Whose worth's unknown, although his height be taken.

Love is not Time's fool, though rosy lips and cheeks

Within his bending sickle's compass come.

Love alters not with his brief hours and weeks,

But bears it out even to the edge of doom.

If this be error and upon me proved,

I never writ, nor no man ever loved.

⌐ What You Want to Remember ⌐

- Just because you lost your money doesn't mean you lost everything. Don't stress what you lack; emphasize what still remains.

- Look around you and take note of the misfortunes of others. Then realize how foolish you are for whining about your cursed fate.

- Those who are wise have always known that the blessings of children, family, and love far outweigh all financial aspects of life.

■ Repeat to yourself every day the teaching of the Jewish classic, *Ethics of the Fathers*: "Who is rich? He who is satisfied with his portion in life."

Notes

1. Maurice McGhea, "The World Is Mine," *Living Better On-Line Magazine,* November 8, 2000.
2. Francine Klagsbrun, *Married People: Staying Together in an Age of Divorce* (New York: Bantam Books, July 1985).

CHAPTER 10

Did the Money Really Buy You Happiness?

It's pretty hard to tell what
does bring happiness.
Poverty and wealth have both failed.

—Kin Hubbard,
twentieth-century author,
humorist, and artist

The German philosopher Robert Spaemann, in an essay on the happy life, points out that, "What happiness consists of has always been debated. Augustin counted 289 views of happiness. The only thing we know is that all humans want to be happy."

Spaemann follows that observation with the wisdom of the Jewish joke about the son who tells his father that he wants to marry Sarah Katz. The father objects because Miss Katz has no dowry. The son insists that only with Sarah will he be happy. Thereupon the father says, "To be happy!—And what good will that do you?"

Happiness is the goal of all mankind, yet it often eludes us. Very often we think that happiness has passed us by, but found a home in almost everyone else's heart. Perhaps the first major truth we ought to acknowledge is the insight Dennis

73

Prager quotes in his wonderful book, *Happiness Is a Serious Problem*, from the mother of his dear friend, the author Joseph Telushkin. Telushkin's mother, Helen, a homemaker and self-described common-sense philosopher, remarked, "The only happy people I know are people I don't know well."

Our first problem with happiness is that we compare ourselves to others and are fooled into believing, by their outward façade of well-being, that they are really happy. Which of course makes us even more unhappy than we were before.

Ever notice the difference between portrait photographs taken a century ago and those taken today? In the old photos, people rarely if ever smiled for the camera. It didn't occur to them that they always had to look happy. Life was serious—and so were they. It didn't seem rational to put on a smile "on the count of three" or just because they heard the word "cheese." Contemporary photographs, however, obey an unwritten rule that everyone must appear to be filled with joy. "Look at me. See how happy I am, how successful I must be—and if that makes you jealous, you just figured out my subconscious motive."

The desire to appear to others always as being happy is in fact one of the greatest reasons for most people's unhappiness. Dale Carnegie, the author of the mega-best-selling *How to Win Friends and Influence People,* recognized this profound truth: "Did you ever see an unhappy horse? Did you ever see birds that had the blues? One reason why birds and horses are not unhappy is because they are not trying to impress other birds and horses." And, he might well have added, other birds and horses don't spend their days trying to retaliate by proving that they are better.

My mother is ninety-eight years old. In Jewish tradition, whenever we mention the age of an elderly person we say "till a hundred and twenty." That was the lifespan of Moses. It wouldn't be nice to ask for more years than the greatest Jew who ever lived so we're satisfied if our loved ones reach his "magic number." Recently I had a long discussion with her and asked her a question that had been on my mind for some time. As a rabbi who has long been involved in marital counseling, I wondered what the secret of my mother's marriage was. My father has been deceased for almost two decades now. My parents' lives were filled with many difficult times. On several occasions, they had to flee their residences for fear of their lives—Poland to Germany to Hungary to Switzerland. Ultimately, they came to the United States where for many years they faced difficult financial struggles. "How is it," I asked my mother, "that in spite of everything you faced, you never gave in to despair and there was clearly great love between you and Dad?" My mother reflected for a few moments, and then said quite simply: "To tell you the truth, *I never knew that we were supposed to be so happy.*"

We have been duped by our society into believing that only a "smiling face" is acceptable. We have been told by all the advertising agencies, over and over again, that we have a right—no, better put, an obligation—to be happy all the time. And why aren't we happy right now? Only because we lack the particular product they are trying to sell us that we really have to have if we want to be happy. Of course when that doesn't work, they convince us that only "a new and improved version" will make our dreams come true. All we have to do is make a little more money and work just a little harder to be able to afford it. Spend less time with our loved ones, they preach to us, in order to make the money that will allow us to buy more material possessions—so we sacrifice relationships for "success," and family for a 24/7 workplace.

It's about time we faced up to the truth. More things don't mean more happiness. The anonymous line, "Those who say that money can't buy happiness don't know where to shop," may be funny, but it isn't fact. David Myers, professor of psychology at Michigan's Hope College, in his book, *The Pursuit of Happiness: Who Is Happy—and Why?*, quotes a student from an extremely wealthy home: "My parents bought me a Mazda 626. Then one year, my stepfather gave me a sailboat.

Later he bought me my own Windsurfer. Our house has two VCRs and three Hitachi televisions. Do these things make me happy? Absolutely not. I would trade all my family's wealth for a peaceful and loving home."

So now that we're crying over our losses in this beaten-down economic climate, let's review the vicious cycle once more. We want above all to be happy. Our culture keeps telling us that the way to be happy is to have more money. Then we can buy more things that will give us more pleasure. When they don't, we're told that we really need more money to buy bigger and better things, so that's why we have to take on more work and more stress—because then we'll really be happy. And as we see less and less of our family and accumulate more and more possessions, we end up discovering that Benjamin Franklin was right: "He who multiplies riches multiplies tears."

Looking in All the Wrong Places

There's a famous story of a drunk standing under a street lamp carefully searching for something. A policeman comes along, asks him what he's looking for, and the man answers, "My keys." Now they both search. After a while, the policeman wants to know whether the man is sure that he lost his keys here. The drunk answers, "No, not here. I lost them back there—but there it's much too dark to find them."

Foolish? Of course. But a beautiful illustration of a common failing of mankind. We keep looking for things in all the wrong places. We rationalize that "the light is better here," but we never stop to ask ourselves if it's possible that what we're looking for is really in the place where we're searching.

"Before we set our hearts too much upon anything, let us examine how happy they are who possess it." That was the brilliant advice of François Duc de La Rochefoucauld. We set our hearts upon wealth. Why not examine how happy they are who possess it? Is there really a correlation between lack of money and misery, between having and happiness?

Joe Dominguez and Vicki Robin, authors of *Your Money or Your* Life,[1] asked over one thousand people from the United States and Canada to rate themselves on a happiness scale of one (miserable) to five (joyous), with three being "can't complain."

Even Dominguez and Robin were surprised to find there is *no correlation whatsoever* between income and happiness. In fact, people earning between zero to $1,000 a month reported being slightly happier than those whose monthly income exceeded $4,000.

Even though we own more than our parents' generation did, the percentage of Americans describing themselves as "very happy" peaked in 1957. Since then it has remained fairly stable or declined. This, despite the fact that Americans consume twice as much as they did in the 1950s, when the average size of a house was about the same as many two-car garages today.

A great deal of other research suggests that little relationship exists between money and happiness.

"Wealth is like health: Although its absence can breed misery, having it is no guarantee of happiness," summarizes Dr. David Myers, professor of psychology at Michigan's Hope College, in his book, *The Pursuit of Happiness: Who Is Happy and Why*.

"If anything, to judge by soaring rates of depression, the quintupling of the violent crime rate since 1960, the doubling of the divorce rate, and the tripling of the teen suicide rate, we're richer and less happy," says Myers.

"Satisfaction isn't so much getting what you want as wanting what you have. There are two ways to be rich: One is to have great wealth, the other is to have few wants," Myers says. Find ways to make the most of the money that does pass through your hands and never lose sight of all that is far more important than money.

So what is it that has a major influence on happiness? Where should we look if not under the lamp of the wealthy?

Study after study shows that what seems to generate happiness most consistently are religion and marriage. A study of Illinois lottery winners found that a year after their bonanza, they were no happier, on average, than most people, notes Professor Andrew Oswald of Warwick University, near Coventry in Britain. Further, at least for industrial nations, "economic progress buys only a small amount of extra happiness."[2]

Advertisers, journalists, politicians, and others tell us constantly that better economic performance means more happiness for a nation. "We feel we would be more cheery if our boss raised our pay, and assume that countries must be roughly the same," writes Oswald in the *Economic Journal*. But the evidence, he finds, is minimal. "The relevance of economic performance," he notes, "is that it may be a means to an end. That end is not the consumption of beefburgers, nor the accumulation of television sets . . . but rather the enrichment of mankind's feelings of well being. Economic things matter only insofar as they make people happier."[3]

Of course, for poor countries or people, greater income does produce significant and lasting gains in well-being. But in Western industrial nations, prosperity has been rising for a long time without a related increase in happiness. Britain, for example, is twice as rich as in 1960 and three times richer than after World War II. American living standards have also risen enormously. In surveys over the years, though, when Americans are asked about happiness levels—very happy, pretty happy, or not too happy—they don't show much change. Fewer said they were not too happy in 1990 than in 1972, and more said they are pretty happy. But the very happy group has shifted little. "It seems extra income is not contributing dramatically to the quality of people's lives," notes Oswald.[4]

Similarly, reported levels of "satisfaction with life" in Western Europe are only slightly higher than they were twenty years ago. Some countries (Belgium and Ireland, for example) show a drop. Despite higher incomes, suicide rates among men in most Western nations have risen, especially among the richer nations. Such rates are highest among the unemployed and those with marital problems. "Joblessness is a major source of distress," says Oswald. It is not so much the loss of income as the loss of self-esteem. Job satisfaction in the United States and Britain has not increased in the past quarter century, despite higher pay.

So what does promote happiness? Regular attendance at a house of worship—church, temple, or synagogue—for one. Religion may give people a longer perspective, says Oswald. Another favorable factor is marriage. Married men commit suicide only one-third as often as other men. Those who are divorced tend to be less happy, too.

More important, as Oswald and others find, is employment. Human happiness is vulnerable to joblessness. Considering that, "Economic growth should not be a government's primary concern," maintains Oswald. So why do people strive so hard to make more of it? Oswald speculates that it may be a matter of keeping up with the Joneses. "What matters to someone who lives in a rich country is his or her relative income." Or maybe H. L. Mencken defined it more correctly: "Wealth is any income that is at least one hundred dollars more a year than the income of one's wife's sister's income." Now that's really emphasizing *relative* income.

The Bottom of the List

Now, here's a shocker. We've just seen that money doesn't make the top of the list for ensuring happiness. What's utterly amazing is where it does rank in a recent study of college students in the *Journal of Personality and Social Psychology*, published by the American Psychological Association. According to the study, *money is at the bottom of the list of would-be psychological needs that bring happiness and fulfillment.*

In order to be happy, the study subjects most needed to believe they were autonomous and competent, to have self-esteem, and to feel a sense of closeness with others. "I like salary raises just as much as everybody, but I'm sure you can think of people who've left fulfilling jobs to make more money somewhere else and regretted it,'' says Kennon M. Sheldon, a psychologist at the University of Missouri–Columbia and coauthor of the study.

At the bottom on the study's list of factors that bring happiness and well-being were popularity/influence and money/luxury. "People who value money, beauty, and popularity more so than they value intimacy, growth, and community contribution really look a lot less mentally healthy and are a lot more unhappy,'' Sheldon adds. "If you really are financially broke and don't have what you need, you should take care of that. But a lot of us, we keep looking for more and more when we already have enough and it should be more meaningful."

The researchers also concluded that the most satisfying experiences stemmed from fulfillment of the top four needs (*autonomy*—feeling that your activities are self-chosen and self-endorsed; *competence*—feeling that you are effective in your activities; *relatedness*—feeling a sense of closeness with others; and *self-esteem*), and the most unsatisfying experiences corresponded to the lack of those psychological needs. Physical thriving, security, meaning, and pleasure ranked midway between the top four needs and bottom two, which were popularity/influence and money/luxury. Self-esteem was the very top need among Americans.

That's why Theodore Rubin was right: "Happiness does not come from doing easy work, but from the afterglow of satisfaction that comes in the wake of the achievement of a difficult task that demanded our best." When are we most happy? When we are happy with ourselves.

⌐ What You Want to Remember ⌐

- No one is happy all the time; to believe that others are, while you are not, is going to make you even more unhappy.

- Happiness doesn't depend so much on your position as on your disposition.

- Believing that wealth automatically leads to joy is one of the most common errors of mankind. It condemns us to pursue money even as we ignore those parts of life that really give it meaning and joy.

- Studies prove that there is almost no correlation between how much you have and how you feel. Wealth doesn't ensure happiness and the lack of it doesn't mean you're going to be miserable.

- Recent studies of college students conclude that in order to be happy, self-esteem is on the very top of the list and money at the very bottom.

- What you want to remember more than anything else are the words of musician songwriter Bob Conklin: "People want riches; what they need is fulfillment."

Notes

1. Joe Dominguez and Vicki Robin, *Your Money or Your Life* (New York: Penguin USA, 1999).
2. Andrew J. Oswald, "Happiness and Economic Performance," *Economic Journal,* November 1997.
3. Oswald, "Work and Money," *The Christian Science Monitor*, December 15, 1997.
4. Ibid.

Oh No,
Not Chapter Eleven!

Bankruptcy is a legal proceeding
in which you put your money in your pants pocket
and give your coat to the creditors.

—Joey Adams,
author and comedian

Sorry. Chapter 11 is the one thing that doesn't belong in this book.

Bankruptcy is an admission of failure. Reading this book is going to restore your self-esteem and remove the words "Chapter 11" from your vocabulary.

That's why we're moving right on to Chapter 12.

It's God's Fault

*God is the silent partner
in all great enterprises.*

—Abraham Lincoln

Do you believe in God?

According to a recent poll conducted by CNN in conjunction with *USA Today* and the Gallup statisticians, about nine out of ten Americans, 86 percent of them to be exact, affirm that they truly believe in the existence of God. In a similar poll commissioned by the Pew Research Center in 1997, 71 percent of the respondents said they do not doubt the existence of God. Going back to 1987, the figure for believers was 60 percent.

Spirituality and faith seem to have made a mockery of those who predicted four decades ago that, "God is dead." There's a famous Mark Twain story where, upon reading a mistaken obituary about himself in the newspaper, he hastily wrote to the editor, "The report of my death is highly exaggerated." God, too, seems to be having the last laugh as most Americans affirm not only a belief in the Creator but also in miracles and the personal intervention of the Divine in human affairs.

In Jewish tradition, on *Rosh Hashanah*, one of the most powerful prayers recited by Jews around the world proclaims this Jewish New Year as the "Day of Judgment"—the day on which God decides "who will live and who will die, who will become rich and who will become poor."

What we never mentioned till now is the unseen hand of God that directs not only our health but also our wealth. What others call luck or coincidence, believers conclude is a decree from the Almighty.

It's strange that people have very mixed feelings about God's role in their fortunes. As Austrian playwright Arthur Schnitzler put it so well: "We know of some very religious people who came to doubt God when a great misfortune befell them, even when they themselves were to blame for it; but we have never yet seen anyone who lost his faith because an undeserved fortune fell to his lot."

People of faith are perfectly willing to attribute both their good and bad fortune to the will of God. Good times are blessings from a Higher Power. Tough times are divine decrees that we may not be able to understand but still have to accept as decisions from a superior intelligence. Granted, God's reasoning is often unclear, but that doesn't make it unjust.

The Lost Million Dollars

A friend of mine shared with me the story of what happened to his father many years ago. His father had owned a stock for a number of years. It went up by several points and he decided to take his profit. Three days later came the announcement that the stock was being taken over, and the price almost tripled. The money my friend's father would have made had he not sold was over a $1 million back in the days when that sum was truly a fortune.

How did this man of faith react to the windfall that eluded him by a matter of days? My friend assures me that not once, for the rest of his life, did he ever voice a regret. "Clearly it was God's will that I not be tested by having great wealth." Belief in a Higher Power allows us to not only be grateful for the good we are blessed with, but also to be accepting of the difficulties that often confront us.

If we're lucky, we can sometimes understand in retrospect why things worked out the way they did. The problem, as Danish philosopher and theologian Søren Kierkegaard so aptly put it, is that "life can only be understood backwards, but it must be lived forward."

We see our portfolios plummet, and we say, "It just doesn't make sense." Yet, even Albert Einstein, who didn't consider himself a religious person, affirmed that, "I cannot believe that God plays dice with the Cosmos." Believers are willing to go a step further: I can't believe that God plays dice with the lives of His children.

The Pay-Back in Warsaw

One of the most memorable experiences of my life demonstrated to me the truth of God's personal financial intervention.

On a trip to Eastern Europe to visit the places where my ancestors lived, as well as the concentration camps where much of my family perished, I spent one Sabbath morning in a synagogue in Warsaw. The custom is for a few people in the congregation to be given the great honor of coming up to the Torah (first you step on to a raised platform, where on a small tabletop the Torah is laid out open) and reciting the appropriate blessings. I didn't identify myself as a rabbi but for some reason, of all the tourists as well as local residents, they selected me as one of the seven designated honorees.

It is also the custom for the people given this honor to publicly make a pledge of a donation for the synagogue. As I concluded my blessings and was emotionally overcome by the realization of where I was and how many great Jewish leaders must have preceded me standing at this very spot, I felt the need to make a very generous contribution. I hesitated, however, because I didn't want to appear like a rich American tourist who is shaming all the other honorees whose contributions were limited by their poverty. As a compromise in my own mind between these conflicting desires, I decided that a pledge of thirty-six American dollars would be just about right—enough to be meaningful as a gift and not exorbitant as an expression of ego. No sooner was the pledge announced than there was an audible gasp from the congregants. It seems that thirty-six American dollars was quite a fortune in the currency of Polish *zlotys*. The president quickly came over to me, asked where I was staying, and if it would be all right for a committee to come to my hotel immediately after the Sabbath to collect this generous donation. Of course I agreed, and within five minutes after the Sabbath ended with the appearance of three stars in the heavens, a committee of three appeared in the lobby and asked me to make good on my pledge. I happily gave them the money and felt very pleased that I had the merit of being able to perform a good deed, a *mitzvah*.

My wife and I then wondered what there was to do to while away a few hours on a Saturday night in Warsaw. The concierge told us there was a casino on the premises and that was about the only activity available to us.

New to gambling, I stopped at the very first slot machine and, on a lark, deposited one coin. What followed was indescribable. Lights flashed, gongs went off, people around the room stopped what they were doing to see what had happened. I stood amazed as money kept pouring out of the machine. It seems that I hit the jackpot, and I quickly kept filling bucket after bucket with my winnings. I immediately decided that I must have used up my share of good luck for that night, and I went to cash in my winnings.

The cashier put all the coins through her counting machine and finally came up with a total. The sum she told me was staggering, and for a moment I thought I was almost a millionaire. What I had forgotten was that the amount she told me was in Polish currency, *zlotys*. Anxiously, I asked her, "What does that come to in American dollars?"

After some quick calculating, she replied, "Oh, about thirty-six American dollars."

For years I had preached that whatever we give eventually comes back to us. But this time God made it so abundantly clear that my contribution was rewarded by its exact equivalent. I had heard similar stories from others and always found them hard to believe. Now I knew first-hand that God is to be found not only in synagogues and houses of worship, but even in Las Vegas, Atlantic City, and a casino in Warsaw!

Don't Tell God–Just Ask

Let me remind you, though, that the Bible teaches us not only that "the Lord giveth" but also that "the Lord taketh."

There is a beautiful parable told about two monks who needed the help of God. One of them said, "I need oil." He planted an olive sapling and prayed, "Lord, it needs rain, that its roots may drink and swell. Please send gentle showers." And the Lord sent a gentle shower. "Lord," the monk prayed again, "my tree needs sun." And the sun shone. "Now, frost, my Lord, to grace its tissues," said the monk, and the little tree sparkled with frost. But as soon as the evening came, the sapling died.

The monk told his colleague of his disappointing experience. "I, too, have planted a little tree," he said, "and it thrives very well. I entrusted my tree to God. I also prayed. What I said was, 'Lord, please send what it needs. Storm or sunshine, wind or frost. You have made it and you know what is best for it.'"

Our problem is not that we pray to God, but that we are too specific. "Please make Cisco go up ten points. Please help me get my job back. Please make my mutual funds recover." What we ought to be saying is, "Please, God, do what you know will eventually be in my best interest." In the biblical book Ecclesiastes, Solomon reminds us that "for everything there is a time and a season." And just as there is a time for peace and a time for war, there is a time in our lives for wealth and another time for us to be humbled by its disappearance.

The Little Girl's Doll

It happened in Hebrew school. The teacher told me the details. Little Sarah, all of six years old, held her broken doll in her hands and prayed fervently to God to fix it. Sammy, the class clown, started to make fun of her. "Do you really think that God listens to you and that He will answer your prayers?"

Sarah was not discouraged and continued with her prayers. The very next day Sammy mockingly walked over to her, saw the doll that was still broken, and said, "Well, I guess I was right. God didn't listen to you."

"Oh, no, of course God listened to my prayers. He answered them, too—it's just that He said 'no.' "

God doesn't always have to give us the answers *we* want. As the Jewish philosopher, Bahya Ibn Pakuda, said: "If I could understand God, I would *be* God." Sometimes God's answer to us is "no" because *that's what's best for us at the time.* It's even possible that God says no just to test us—before saying yes. As Lusin (Lu Xun), regarded as China's greatest writer of the twentieth century, writes in his epigrams: "When God wishes to send disaster upon a person, He first sends him a little success to elate him and see whether he can receive it in a worthy manner. When God wishes to send blessing upon a person, He first sends him a little misfortune and sees how well he can take it."

If you believe that God is capable of running the entire universe, then you've got to believe He's capable of overseeing the global economy as well as Nasdaq, the New York Stock Exchange, AMEX—and even the company you work for (or the one that is soon going to hire you). What happened to you wasn't caused by Alan Greenspan. Trust me. Even Greenspan isn't as great as God.

And God does really care about you—even when you think he's ignoring you!

⟶ What You Want to Remember ⟵

- Belief in God makes it a lot easier to accept our fate. It's not the Dow Jones but divine decree that governs our lives.

- Most Americans believe in a personal God. Sometimes He gives, and sometimes He takes away—and sometimes He leaves us signs of His involvement.

- It's not our place to advise God how to best manage our affairs. Just as in marriage, our contract is "for better or for worse."

- All of us need to constantly remind ourselves of the words of Woodrow Wilson: "I firmly believe in Divine Providence. Without belief in Providence, I think I should go crazy. Without God, the world would be a maze without a clue."

CHAPTER 13

Is There Life After Failure?

*Failure is success
if we learn from it.*

—Malcolm Forbes

If you've lost money in the stock market or watched your career crumble in this bad economy, I have some great news for you. According to a recent report in *The Wall Street Journal*, people who are financial failures are now "in" and earning as much as $10,000 a pop by giving motivational speeches talking about their lack of success!

Who would believe it? "Losers" are in demand. And what could possibly explain this strange phenomenon? According to one expert quoted by the *Journal*, the dot-com failures have wiped out so many people's fortunes and derailed so many careers, that victims are seeking inspiration from individuals who have survived similar disasters! Listening to how others screwed up, people feel less devastated by their own mistakes.

Searching for "Failures"

People who failed have not only become popular as speakers. They're even courted by major companies because they feel that those who have failed once have learned far more from

90

their experience than those who so far have only been blessed with success and never had to rise after falling.

Bill Coleman, founder and chief executive of one of the most effective tech start-ups, BEA Systems, explains that Silicon Valley's investment philosophy has changed in the five years his company has been operating. Now the consensus is that there are three experiences every member of a founding business should have: First, they have to have worked as an executive with a large company. "If you ever hear an entrepreneur say he doesn't like large companies and that's why he started his own, you say 'go and talk to somebody else because you're never going to run a big company.'" The second thing to look for is experience working with a start-up. The third, the most unexpected and yet perhaps the most important, is the experience of failure—not necessarily a whole company, but even a project. "You don't know how you're going to react as an executive to a failure."

And Coleman should know. He had two failed ventures behind him before he started BEA Systems. Today, the man who failed twice is founder and chief executive of a company with market capitalization of more than $28 billion. Coleman proves the truth of Winston Churchill's observation: "Success is the ability to go from one failure to another with no loss of enthusiasm."

Failing and Failure

S. I. Hayakawa, former U.S. senator from California and a specialist in semantics, alerted us to an all-important distinction between two English words that most of us assume are identical: "Notice the difference between what happens when a man says to himself, 'I have failed three times,' and what happens when he says, 'I am a failure.'" To think of yourself as a failure is to create a perpetual self-image as a loser. W. C. Fields suggested, "If at first you don't succeed, try, try again. Then quit. There's no use being a damn fool about it." But W. C. Fields was not a philosopher. He was a comedian who couldn't quit, at least when it came to drinking and destroying himself. Confucius, who *was* a philosopher, observed that, "Our greatest glory is not in never falling, but in rising every time we fall."

If you learn from your experience, if your failure inspires you to surpass yourself and to do it better next time, if you understand that failure is merely a momentary event but never defines a person—then you are an alumnus of the best school in the world, and your failure was the tuition you paid for your eventual success.

Meet Some "Failures" Who Weren't

In *U.S. News and World Report* (February 20, 2000), the results of a survey of fifty-eight of the most prominent historians in the world was published. The question to which they responded was, "Who in your opinion is the greatest of all American presidents?" Almost unanimously, the declared winner was the sixteenth president of the United States—Abraham Lincoln. Did you know that Honest Abe lost every election he entered—except for the last one? Just imagine how different American history would be if, after failing numerous times, Abraham Lincoln had given up trying!

Gail Devers, a three-time Olympic gold medallist in track and field, holds the title of "Fastest Woman in the World." In 1992, she won the 100-meter dash at the Olympics in record-breaking time. What most people didn't know is that just one year earlier she had been two days away from having both her feet amputated. When, in 1988, after the Olympic games in Seoul, Korea, her performance plummeted, she was diagnosed with Graves' disease, a thyroid dysfunction marked by an overactive and enlarged thyroid gland. After extensive medical treatment, she returned to competition, and then ran successfully in the 1992 Olympics. A year later, at the 1993 world championships in Stuttgart, Germany, Gail won gold medals in both the 100-meter dash and the 100-meter hurdles, an accomplishment that had not been achieved in forty-five years. She, too, failed for a brief time—but she was not a failure.

Ever hear of a country's political leader who, just a few decades ago, was run out of office and labeled an alcoholic who suffered fits of depression? He failed and his political career in Israel came to an inglorious end. Yet, Yitzchak Rabin chose not to accept temporary failure as final verdict. Instead, years later he returned as Prime Minister, to international acclaim. His success could never be terminated by lack of self-will, but only by the bullet of an assassin. Most prominent world leaders came to pay him homage at his funeral. To the man who once failed, the President of the United States, Bill Clinton, tearfully bade farewell with the now-famous words, "*Shalom, chaver*—(Goodbye, friend)."

Let me introduce you to one other loser turned winner who is not nearly as famous. I wouldn't be surprised if you have never heard of Maxey Filer. Maxey Filer had one dream in life. More than anything else, he wanted to become a lawyer. He took the Bar examination in California and failed. So he took it again. And he failed. For twenty-four years, Maxey Filer took the Bar examination in California twice a year—and failed it every time. But in 1998, on his forty-ninth attempt, he finally passed. At the age of sixty-one, when he was sworn in as a lawyer, he got a standing ovation from his colleagues. They were applauding a man who showed us that motivational speaker Zig Zigler was right in saying, "Failure is a detour, not a dead end street."

Believe It or Not–Even Billionaires "Failed"

George Soros is widely considered to be the most successful investor of our times—and according to some, of all time. As a billionaire many times over, he has been both deified and vilified, called a shark and a saint. The Hungarian-born financier went from hunted Jew in his homeland during World War II to become the founder and controlling genius behind a business empire based in New York, known as Quantum Fund.

His speculative coups are the stuff of legends. Betting on the rise or fall of major currencies, he outwitted the Bank of England and the brilliant bankers of Europe. On many days his profits exceeded the annual budgets of quite a few countries. His aides watched in awe as he would confidently wager hundreds of millions of dollars on a single position.

More often than not, his decisions proved to be right. *But inevitably there were times when it turned out that he was spectacularly wrong!*

Following Black Monday on October 19, 1987, when the stock market crashed with a vengeance not seen since 1929, Soros became extremely bearish. On what has since become known as Terrible Tuesday—in great measure precipitated by Soros' over-reaction—the market tumbled once more in the morning as the supposedly far-sighted prophet mercilessly dumped S&P 500 futures. Not only did the market recover later in the day, but *it never again traded much lower.*

After the fall of communism, Soros jumped into the Russian market. It was a move that would cost him *$2 billion* when the Russian economy collapsed in 1998. Compounding this costly misjudgment, Soros confided that this episode inspired him to write his book, *The Crisis of Global Capitalism,* which predicted the imminent collapse of the capitalistic system. Soros, to his credit, has publicly admitted that he lived to eat his words and that his work leaves him with "egg on his face."

If you're starting to feel sorry for this terrible "failure," please be reassured that you won't have to hold any fundraisers for him in the foreseeable future. To this day, Soros remains an immensely wealthy man, a major philanthropist, and a prominent financial figure whose opinions are sought by some of the most powerful people in the world.

But what about those incredible errors of judgment? In

an interview with *The New York Times*, Soros gave the best explanation: "Basically, I got carried away. I goofed."

What a powerful message for all of us to remember! Soros goofed. But guess what? Whether he ever heard it or not, he instinctively knew, as Henry Ford put it, that "Failure is only the opportunity to begin again more intelligently." No one, no matter how brilliant, is immune from mistakes. Failing is the price we pay for being "only human." Failures are the people who forget that they can still be hugely successful in spite of their mortal limitations.

So now, let me ask you a question. You're down on yourself and you're deeply disturbed by your investment blunders. You know that you goofed. How are you dealing with it? Do you think that you failed—or that you are a failure?

The irony is that whichever answer you chose, you'll prove to be right!

The Two Kinds of People

We love to categorize people, usually by labeling them by one of two distinctly different characteristics. People are skinny or fat, introverted or extroverted, optimists or pessimists, serious or funny. All of these lead to stereotyping and to generalizations that aren't completely accurate.

There is one division of people, however, that Benjamin Barber, a political scientist at Rutgers University, teaches that may summarize an ultimate truth about human behavior. Barber was asked his opinion of the common division of people into successes and failures. His insights deserve not only to be quoted, but to be observed and committed to memory by every one of us:

> I don't divide the world into the weak and the strong, or the
> successes and the failures, those who make it or those who
> don't. I don't even divide the world into the extroverted and
> the introverted, or those who hear the inner voice or the
> outer voice, because we all hear some of both.

I divide the world into learners and nonlearners.

There are people who learn, who are open to what happens around them, who listen, who hear the lessons. When they do something stupid, they don't do it again. When they do something that works a little bit, they do it even better and harder the next time.

The question to ask is not whether you are a success or a failure, but whether you are a learner or a nonlearner.

If I can summarize what he said in one sentence, it's this: "If we learn from an experience, there is no such thing as failure."

Seniority Versus Experience

Two men worked in a large office. One had been there as manager for twenty years. The other, in an almost identical capacity, had joined the firm just three years before. Unexpectedly, the death of a vice president created an opening with far greater authority, status, and salary. Both men desperately wanted the job. The CEO, after great deliberation, gave the good news of his appointment to the employee who had been with the firm for only three years.

The overlooked candidate, deeply hurt, came to complain. "How could you do this," he said to the CEO, "when I have so much more experience than he has?"

"No," the CEO responded, "he has more experience than you."

"How can that possibly be, if I've been here twenty years and he's been here only three?"

"Simple," said the CEO. "He has three years' experience. You have one year's experience twenty times over."

Experience means nothing if we learn nothing from it. As Aldous Huxley put it, "Experience is not what happens to a man; it is what a man does with what happens to him."

Getting Personal

There's a famous story about a preacher who, before he started his sermon, told the congregation that he was going to be very critical but he didn't want anybody to feel offended. "Whatever failings and sins I'm going to talk about really apply to me. I'm actually trying to improve myself—but since you're all sitting here, I'll speak a little louder."

To be honest, that's exactly what I think right now as I reflect on my own experience. As a professional speaker and lecturer I've never found it difficult to address audiences of thousands. It's only when I look at myself in the mirror that I feel apprehensive about giving advice. After all, it may be true that you can fool all of the people some of the time—but if you include yourself in the group you're misleading then you are surely the greatest fool of all!

Where do I stand in the class of victims of this tough economy? Has my experience made me better or merely bitter? Did I learn from my mistakes and gain anything from my misfortune—or am I now simply poorer and none the wiser?

I'd like to believe that adversity has served as my most insightful teacher. Experience has granted me previously unknown revelations. Yes, I lost a great deal of money—but I gained a new "me." My lessons may have been costly, but they brought with them a kind of understanding more precious than gold.

Today I know that:

- Playing the market is much different from being an investor.

- Pride is another word for stupidity if you claim credit for profits temporarily created by a bull market run wild.

- Paper profits are the illusion of wealth created by the myopia of greed.

- Margin is a seductive temptress more enticing than Delilah—and far more dangerous.

- Money doesn't *make* people better; it just allows them to *become* kinder and more charitable.

- Losing money doesn't mean you're a fool, just as making a fortune doesn't prove you're a genius.

- Maturity means knowing how to cope with failure—and with success.

- The market respects those who treat it seriously and research it thoroughly; it mocks those who think its rewards are freely granted to the followers of friendly tips and excited phone calls from "helpful" strangers.

- Just as in every other game of chance, all of your winnings should *never* be left on the table.

- The law of gravity was not repealed for the sake of Wall Street; even there the rule still holds that "whatever goes up must come down."

- My annual salary and my soul aren't identical; I *am* more than what I *own*.

- Forgiveness is a virtue even to myself; I can forgive the fact that I failed—because I know that I am not a failure.

- And finally, as I begin anew with faith and with confidence, I know as surely as day follows night that "It ain't over till the fat lady sings"—and I thankfully haven't seen or heard from her in the slightest.

Why Vince Lombardi Was Wrong

There's hardly a person who doesn't know the famous motto of Vince Lombardi, former coach of the Green Bay Packers: "Winning isn't everything—it's the *only* thing."

Unfortunately, all too many people apply this standard not just to football but to everything in life.

What's the worst thing you can say to someone today? "You're a loser!" That's why every failure becomes traumatic. Every setback becomes internalized and causes loss of self-esteem. Reversals aren't opportunities in disguise, but final judgments on our intelligence.

For the sake of our children, our society, and our personal sanity, we have to get over the Vince Lombardi syndrome. Winning is *not* the only thing. Sometimes it's even the wrong thing.

- We have got to give our children *permission to fail*. If you give them the message that failing even once turns you into a failure, you will create a self-fulfilling prophecy.

- Failure allows us to take risks. French statesman George S. Clemenceau reminded us that, "A man's life is interesting precisely when he has failed. I well know. For it's a sign he tried to surpass himself."

- Failure teaches us compassion and humility. If winning is everything, then losing makes you a nothing. Winners can therefore treat you with the disdain they think you deserve. Humility is hardly possible when you're sure you're a genius because you tapped into a bull market. To get back these qualities that make us truly human, it might even prove to be a blessing when we suffer a financial setback.

- Failure allows us to dare what we might never have tried if we felt the need to repeat previous success. Pulitzer Prize winner Tennessee Williams' first play was a huge failure. He later confessed that if he had not had this failure, he would never have written *The Glass Menagerie*. That's how many Holocaust survivors have told me they explain success they achieved after World War II, although they started with nothing when they were liberated: "When I tried something new and daring, I asked myself what could conceivably happen? I wasn't afraid of the worst possibility coming true because I had already lived through the worst—and survived."

- Failure lets us know who our friends really are. Fair-weather friends suddenly disappear when you've lost your fortune. Those who liked you only because of what you could do for them no longer stab you in the back; even the front is permissible. Discovering who is a true friend that stays loyal even in your time of need is a revelation that's worth far more than money.

- Finally, failure spurs us to review our priorities, to reflect on our goals, and to rekindle the spiritual side of our souls that was temporarily stilled by our monetary obsession.

How Losing Is Winning

Perhaps the best way to refute Vince Lombardi's credo that, "Winning isn't everything—it's the *only* thing," is with a story that happened just recently at a fund-raising dinner for Chush, a school that serves learning-disabled children.

The father of one of the school's students delivered a speech that would never be forgotten. After extolling the school and its dedicated staff, he offered a question. "Everything God does is done with perfection. Yet, my son, Shai, cannot learn things as other children do. He cannot understand things as other children do. Where is God's plan reflected in my son?" The audience was stilled by the query. The father continued. "I believe," the father answered, "that when God brings a child like Shai into the world, an opportunity to realize the Divine Plan presents itself. And it comes in the way people treat that child." Then he told the following story:

> During the week, Shai attends Chush together with other children who have learning disabilities. On Sundays, though, Shai participates in an integrated program with nonchallenged boys. As Shai's father came to pick him up one Sunday, some of his classmates had begun a game of pick-up baseball. Shai asked, "Do you think they will let me

play?" Shai's father knew that most boys would not want him on their team. But the father understood that if his son were allowed to play it would give him a much-needed sense of belonging. Shai's father approached one of the boys on the field and asked if Shai could play. The boy looked around for guidance from his teammates. Getting none, he took matters into his own hands and said, "We are losing by six runs, and the game is in the eighth inning. I guess he can be on our team and we'll try to put him up to bat in the ninth inning." In the bottom of the eighth inning, Shai's team scored a few runs but was still behind by three. At the top of the ninth inning, Shai put on a glove and played in the outfield. Although no hits came his way, he was obviously ecstatic just being on the field, grinning from ear to ear as his father waved to him from the stands. In the bottom of the ninth inning, Shai's team scored again. Now, with two outs and the bases loaded, the potential winning run was on base. Shai was scheduled to be the next at bat. Would the team actually let Shai bat at this juncture and give away their chance to win the game? Surprisingly, Shai was given the bat. Everyone knew that a hit was all but impossible because Shai didn't even know how to hold the bat properly, much less connect with the ball. However, as Shai stepped up to the plate, the pitcher moved a few steps to lob the ball in softly so Shai could at least be able to make contact. The first pitch came and Shai swung clumsily and missed. The pitcher again took a few steps forward to toss the ball softly toward Shai. As the pitch came in, Shai swung at the ball and hit a slow ground ball to the pitcher. The pitcher picked up the soft grounder and could easily have thrown the ball to the first baseman. Shai would have been out and that would have ended the game. Instead, the pitcher took the ball and threw it on a high arc to right field, far beyond reach of the first baseman. Everyone started yelling, "Shai, run to first, run to first." Never in his life had Shai made it to first base. He scampered down the baseline, wide-eyed and startled. Everyone yelled, "Run to second, run to second!" By the time Shai was rounding first base, the right fielder had the ball. He could have thrown the ball to the second baseman for a tag. But the right fielder understood what the pitcher's intentions had been, so he threw the ball high and far over the third baseman's head. Shai ran toward second base as the runners ahead of him deliriously circled the bases toward home. As Shai reached second base, the opposing shortstop ran to him, turned him in the direction of third base, and shouted, "Run to third!" As Shai rounded third, the boys from both teams were screaming, "Shai! Run home!" Shai ran home, stepped on home plate, and was cheered as the hero for hitting a "grand slam" and winning the game for his team.

"That day," said the father softly with tears now rolling down his face, "the boys from both teams helped bring a piece of the Divine Plan into this world." And some people would be stupid enough to say that the team Shai played with were really the losers!

⎯ What You Want to Remember ⎯

■ The "F" word that is most obscene is "Failure." People who fail aren't failures. They've simply taken the first step to success.

■ Failure is the best form of feedback and learning experience—which is why some of the largest corporations seek leaders from among those who have already graduated from the School of Hard Knocks.

■ Failing doesn't turn you into a failure—unless you truly believe that it does.

■ The world is not divided into successes and failures, but into learners and nonlearners. To learn from having failed is to turn a curse into a blessing.

■ Failing, even financially, can bring with it many benefits. Whereas our material goods may be diminished, our spiritual stature and our divine qualities of compassion, kindness, and humility can find far greater expression.

■ Some of the greatest people in history failed and then proved, by their determination and their refusal to accept the finality of defeat, that instead of being failures they could become President of the United States, an Olympic medallist, and even a billionaire.

■ Vince Lombardi was wrong. Playing to lose can sometimes be the greatest moral victory.

CHAPTER 14

Are You Being Tested?

The gem cannot be polished without friction,
nor man perfected without trials.

—Confucius

The Book of Job is the one book in the Bible that most acutely deals with the problem of man's suffering. Professor George Foot Moore of Harvard University summarized the universal appeal and relevance of this work in these words: "The Book of Job is the greatest work of Hebrew literature that has come down to us, and one of the great poetical works of the world's literature."

The story speaks to anyone who has had to confront tragedy in his life—and therefore its message is directed to all of mankind.

Most of us are familiar with the book. Job is introduced to us as a man of exemplary virtue and piety. God blesses him with lavish material possessions and with an ideal family, seven sons and three daughters. Inexplicably, Job is suddenly smitten with a series of calamities. First to go is his wealth. Next, he loses his children. Through all of this, Job still holds on to his faith and expresses the words that would be repeated by believers throughout the generations: "The Lord hath given, and the Lord hath taken away; blessed be the name of the Lord.''

Job's friends come to visit and insist that he must have sinned. Search your soul, they tell him, because there's no way that this could happen to a righteous person. Their theology is limited to the simplistic view that affliction is a certain proof of sin. Job knows he's innocent and that the accusations of his friends are wrong. ''I am innocent,'' Job cries out, ''I regard not myself, I despise my life'' (Job 9:21). Job knows he has done no wrong. Still, when Job's wife loses faith and urges him euphemistically to ''bless'' God and die, Job rebukes her: ''What? Shall we receive good at the hand of God and shall we not receive evil?'' Job rejects her advice to renounce God just because his life is now filled with suffering. He remembers all the good he enjoyed in the past and can't give up trusting in the God who so often showered him with love and with blessings.

As Tennyson put it, the Book of Job ''is our first, oldest statement of the never-ending problem—man's destiny and God's ways with him here in this earth.'' If God is good, why is life so unfair? Only those who can successfully deal with this apparent proof of the absence of Divine Providence can even in the worst of times proclaim with Job, ''But as for me, I know that my Redeemer lives'' (19:25).

What Job Didn't Know

Job is a book that allows the reader, at the very outset, far more information than is granted to the protagonist. In a dramatic prologue, God proudly points out Job to the celestial beings as an example of the spiritual heights humans can achieve. Satan seizes this opportunity to cast the suspicion of doubt on Job's virtue. ''Of course,'' Satan argues, ''Job is today your faithful servant. But that is only because You have 'blessed the work of his hands, and his possessions are increased in the land. But put forth Your hand now and touch

all that he has, surely he will blaspheme Thee to Thy face'"
(1:10–11).

God, confident of the outcome of this test of faith, accepts
the challenge and allows Satan to shower misfortunes upon
His trusting follower. When financial loss followed by the
death of his children fail to cause Job to curse God, Satan asks
for permission to increase Job's travails by bringing harm to
"Job's very bone and flesh." God allows even this, imposing
only one last condition: "Spare his life."

The reader knows all along that the explanation of the
friends of Job is not only cruel but also wrong. Job is in fact a
pious and holy man. His suffering had nothing to do with sin.
From the book's opening, we are aware that Job isn't being
punished, he is being tested. The test will give him the opportunity to prove his true character.

Why Does God Test, When He Already Knows?

How could God's purpose have been to test Job? God is omniscient. Wouldn't He already know what would happen?

What is the point of all the other stories in the Bible, as
well, where the Lord puts people to a test? In Genesis, God
tells Abraham to offer up his son, his only son that he loves so
dearly, as a sacrifice. No, of course, God doesn't mean it.
Human sacrifice is considered a heinous crime in the Bible.
God was just testing Abraham, to determine the strength of
his commitment, but He never wanted this command to be
carried out. At the very last moment, when the horrible deed
is about to be done, God sends an angel to stop Abraham from
completing his task. It's almost as if, after days of Abraham's
inner torment, God appears just in the nick of time to tell him,
"Oh, I was just kidding. I never meant for you to actually offer
up your child on the altar."

What's missing here too is an explanation of why God
would make someone endure a most difficult test if He already
knows the outcome in advance?

The answer may well provide us with a deeper understanding not only of the travails of Job and Abraham, but even
of the problems that we ourselves have confronted in our own
lives.

The Benefits of Adversity

There is a legend of a comfort-loving man who died and was
borne to the other world where every wish was gratified. No
effort, no struggle was required of him. He became bored and
said, "I can't stand this everlasting bliss any longer. I want to
feel there are things I cannot have. I want to go to Hell." The
attendant replied: "And where do you think you are, sir?"

We think of adversity as a curse. To view it as a test is to
understand that it is not God who needs to know whether we
will overcome, but it is we, through our suffering, who have
to realize what it is we are capable of learning from our misfortunes so that we can mature and find greatness. The famous
historian, Will Durant, considered this one of the most important lessons of history: "Rome remained great as long as she
had enemies who forced her to unity, vision, and heroism.
When she had overcome them all, she flourished for a moment and then began to die."

I can hardly imagine anyone more afflicted than Helen Keller. Yet, it is she who said with conviction, "I thank God for
my handicaps, for, through them, I have found myself, my
work, and my God."

So, too, for those of us who cry over lost fortunes, it's important to listen to the advice of one of the greatest financial
geniuses. Bernard Baruch said that the blessing he had to
learn in order not only to make but to keep a great fortune is
that, "The art of living lies not in eliminating but in growing
with troubles."

What Nature Teaches Us

If we look around us carefully, we can learn profound truths
from the workings of nature that surely apply to us as well.

Poet and author LeRoy V. Brant described an experience that changed his entire outlook on life.

One of Brant's childhood hobbies was to collect the cocoons of the Cecropia moth. He tells how much he loved to watch the moths struggle to escape from the confinement of their cocoons and to fly away. One day, his father cut the imprisoning silk away from one such creature, helping it to emerge. In no time, the moth tried to flutter its wings and fly but was unable to do so. It fell to the ground, dead.

His father explained to him, "The struggle a moth makes to come out of the cocoon drives the poison from its body. If that poison is not driven out, the moth will die."

Brant concluded that what was true for the moth is just as true for mankind. When people struggle for what they want, they become stronger and better. But if things come too easily, they become weak, and something in them seems to die.[1]

How to Make Pearls

Nature gives us yet another example that teaches a similar message. Would you believe that something as low in the evolutionary chain as an oyster can offer us profound insight? The most extraordinary thing about the oyster is what it does when irritations get into its shell. It doesn't like them. It attempts to get rid of them. But when it finds itself incapable of doing that, it settles down to make of them one of the most beautiful things in the world. It uses the irritation to do the loveliest thing that an oyster ever has the chance to do: It turns its irritation into a pearl.

Isn't that a prescription for happiness for all of us? Irritations come in many forms. They range from troubles to tragedies. What we have to learn is to discover the secret of transforming our difficulties into pearls as well.

Turning Grief into Greatness

See if you can possibly guess what these business titans have in common: Rupert Murdoch, Ted Turner, Craig McCaw, Thomas

Monahan of Domino's Pizza, Chase dealmaker Jimmy Lee, First Amendment lawyer Martin Garbus, and Tampa Bay Buccaneers owner Malcolm Glazer.

Want a hint? More than half of British prime ministers as well as such U.S. Presidents as Washington, Jefferson, Lincoln, FDR, Cleveland, and Clinton are in the same category.

Give up? A fascinating study conducted by Harvard social scientist Phyllis Silverman (as reported in FORBES of April 16, 2001) determined that while less than ten percent of the population loses a parent at a young age in modern times, all of these great leaders and super-successful businessmen suffered this fate.

Kenneth Doka, who teaches death studies at New Rochelle College, explains the connection this way: The death of a parent gives the child an unfortunate but critical developmental push. Some will be crushed by the responsibility of becoming family caretakers, while others will integrate this role into their personalities and be spurred on.

Gary Winnick, the billionaire entrepreneur, lost his father when he was eighteen years old. As he sees it, this tragedy transformed him overnight and gave him the overwhelming determination to succeed. "No professional adversity can ever reach the pain I suffered when my father died. Any obstacle thrown in my path becomes a challenge and another hurdle to climb over."

For Ted Turner, "My father's death taught me I never had time to waste." So Turner threw himself totally into the task of building CNN, a media empire he eventually sold to Time Warner for $7.5 billion in 1996.

The founder of Domino's Pizza, Thomas Monahan, grew up in an orphanage after his father died when he was but five years old. He now explains his success with the observation that, "When you have holes in your socks, you'll do anything to be able to afford new ones."

A self-described control freak and workaholic, Chase J.P. Morgan Vice Chairman Jimmy Lee believes that losing his father when he was twelve "energized me to win people over and become my own poster boy for overachievement. Since I didn't have a role model, I created the perfect one."

Martin Garbus, the prominent lawyer whose mother died when he was three, sees it somewhat differently: "Since you never got all the love you needed, you look for external support and confirmation."

Put most succinctly, what all these successful people have in common is the courage and wisdom to build a better life on the foundation of childhood tragedy; not to be defeated by adversity, but to become stronger as a result of coping with its challenges. They achieved not _in spite of_ their grief, but in great measure _because_ of it.

The Broken Violin

Perhaps the best way to illustrate that crises give us the opportunity to demonstrate who we really are is the remarkable story surrounding a concert given by the renowned violinist, Itzhak Perlman. It was on the night of November 18, 1995, that Perlman came on stage to give a concert at Avery Fisher Hall at Lincoln Center in New York City.

If you have ever been to a Perlman concert, you know that getting on stage is no small achievement for him. He was stricken with polio as a child, and so he has braces on both legs and walks with the aid of two crutches. To see him walk across the stage one step at a time, painfully and slowly, is an awesome sight. He walks haltingly, yet majestically, until he reaches his chair.

Then he sits down, slowly, puts his crutches on the floor, undoes the clasps on his legs, tucks one foot back and extends the other foot forward. Then he bends down and picks up the violin, puts it under his chin, nods to the conductor, and proceeds to play. By now, the audience is used to this ritual. They sit quietly while he makes his way across the stage to his chair. They remain reverently silent while he undoes the clasps on his legs. They wait until he is ready to play.

But this time, something went wrong. Just as he finished the first few bars, one of the strings on his violin broke. You could hear it snap—it went off like gunfire across the room. There was no mistaking what that sound meant. There was no mistaking what he had to do.

People who were there that night thought to themselves: "We figured that he would have to get up, put on the clasps again, pick up the crutches and limp his way off stage—to either find another violin or else find another string for this one."

But he didn't. Instead, he waited a moment, closed his eyes and then signaled the conductor to begin again. The orchestra began, and he played from where he had left off. And he played with such passion and such power and such purity as they had never heard before.

Of course, anyone knows that it is impossible to play a symphonic work with just three strings. I know that, and you know that, but that night Itzhak Perlman refused to know that. You could see him modulating, changing, recomposing the piece in his head. At one point, it sounded like he was detuning the strings to get new sounds from them that they had never made before.

When he finished, there was an awesome silence in the room. And then people rose and cheered. There was an extraordinary outburst of applause from every corner of the auditorium. The entire audience was on its feet, screaming and cheering, doing everything they could to show how much they appreciated what he had done.

He smiled, wiped the sweat from his brow, raised his bow to quiet everyone, and then he said—not boastfully, but in a quiet, pensive, reverent tone—"You know, sometimes it is the artist's task to find out how much music you can still make with what you have left."[2]

What a powerful line that is. It has stayed in my mind ever since I read it.

And who knows? Perhaps that is the definition of life—not

just for artists but for all of us. Here is a man who has prepared all his life to make music on a violin of four strings, who, all of a sudden, in the middle of a concert, finds himself with only three strings. So he makes music with three strings And the music he made that night with just three strings was more beautiful, more sacred, more memorable, than any that he had ever made before, when he had four strings.

So, perhaps our task in this shaky, fast-changing, bewildering world in which we live is to make music, at first with all that we have, and then, when that is no longer possible, to make music with what we have left.

Tests and Exams

All of us have had to take exams in school and to confront tests in life. But there is a big difference between them. For exams, you study beforehand. Tests are meant to teach you afterwards.

To really understand that many of our problems are divinely sent tests is to comprehend the wisdom of the renowned U.S. educator Booker T. Washington's observation that "Character is the sum of all we struggle against."

That's why, no matter how much you've lost, you have to find the strength and the wisdom to repeat the immortal words of Job: "The Lord hath given, and the Lord hath taken away. Blessed be the name of the Lord."

─ What You Want to Remember ─

- If we suffer, to any extent, the troubles of Job, we have to consider that from a biblical perspective the reason might be that we're being tested.

- Tests are not meant so that God may know, but rather so that man may grow. In the words of Roman statesman Pliny the Younger, "Prosperity tries the fortunate, adversity the great."

■ Nature demonstrates that from irritations come pearls. Transcending our misfortunes is what permits us to rise to the grandeur of our greatest potential.

■ The author of these lines is unknown but they convey a powerful idea that I suggest you take to heart:

If the sun always shines, there is a desert below.
It takes a little rain to make everything grow.

Notes

1. LeRoy V. Brant, quoted in *Speaker's Book of Illustrative Stories*, Maxwell Droke, editor (Indianapolis: Droke House, 1956), pp. 9–10.
2. Courtesy of Rabbi Jack Riemer, who recorded the story.

CHAPTER 15

Pessimism
Is Deadly

My life has been full of terrible misfortunes,
most of which never happened.

—Michel deMontaigne

"There's no way the market will recover."

"Things can only get worse."

"I'll *never* recoup my losses."

"I guess I won't be able to retire."

"I'll never get a job as good as the one I had."

"So much for Champagne Wishes and Caviar Dreams."

Do these quotes sound like they come from anyone you know? Are they things you might even say yourself? Well, it's time to tell you that of all the "isms" we know—communism, fascism, nazism, terrorism—the only one that kills the soul is pessimism.

Who is a pessimist? Looking at a bagel, he sees the hole and not the bread. A pessimist is a man who thinks that the chief purpose of sunshine is to cast shadows. A pessimist is a misfortune teller. In short, a pessimist is a person who is never happy unless he is miserable.

Perhaps you'll say that the optimist is, in the words of humorist Don Marquis, "a guy who has never had much experience." After all, who can honestly profess that a pessimistic view of the world isn't more realistic? Aren't the optimist and the pessimist both entitled to their opinions?

Perhaps the best answer to these questions is implicit in the way we think of God. Which of the two is the Creator of the universe—an optimist or a pessimist? If we believe the words of the Bible, all we have to do is look at the opening chapter. Every day God created something different and then He figuratively stepped back to evaluate what He had brought into being. What He saw pleased Him greatly, and from day to day he gave His verdict that "it was good." Then, when He finally completed His work with the creation of Adam and Eve, the Bible tells us, "And God saw everything that He had made, and, behold, it was *very* good" (Genesis 1:31).

That's why William James, the American psychologist and philosopher, was right when he said that, "Pessimism is essentially a religious disease." A pessimist disagrees with divine judgment. A pessimist believes that we live in the worst of all possible worlds. Too bad he doesn't take seriously the opinion of the One who made it!

What Happens When You Disagree with God?

People may disagree about almost anything without serious consequences. I like the Mets, you like the Yankees. I thought the movie was wonderful, and you feel it's the biggest stinker you ever saw in your life. Disagreements make life interesting. How boring it would be if we all reacted in exactly the same way to everything.

That's not true, however, for the controversy between optimists and pessimists. Researchers at the Mayo Clinic in Rochester, Minnesota, have confirmed what many people already believed. In a study completed in early 2000, they concluded that optimists tend to live longer and healthier lives. After an extensive and lengthy study with a group of 839 patients who had taken a personality test in the 1960s, they graded the subjects, who ranged in age from eighteen to eighty-four, as optimists or pessimists.

Researchers classified 124 as optimistic, 518 as mixed, and 197 as pessimistic. The study found that the optimists had a better-than-expected survival rate and the pessimists had a 19 percent increase in the risk of death.

The researchers couldn't explain how pessimism is associated with a risk of early death, and suggested a mind–body link, with a "happiness" factor being one of the most important causes of good health.[1]

In yet another study, published by the American Psychological Association, doctors concluded that optimism even played a crucial role in the dreaded illness of cancer. They carefully followed 238 patients with metastasized or recurrent cancer who were receiving radiation treatment for their symptoms. The most prevalent form of cancer among them was cancer of the lung or breast; the least common were colorectal and gastrointestinal cancers. Assessments of the patients' optimism, pessimism, and level of depression were taken when they entered the study and again four months and eight months later. In the interim, seventy patients had died by the eight-month follow-up.

The researchers concluded that there is a definite connection between pessimism and mortality for patients under the age of sixty. They could not explain why at a certain point in life it no longer matters how one views the world. Yet they were unanimous in their conclusion that, "Our findings indicate that the endorsement of a pessimistic life orientation may function as an important risk factor for mortality among younger cancer patients."

Again, the researchers could not explain the precise mechanism by which pessimism affects mortality in cancer patients.

They did offer the suggestion, though, that "it is possible that pessimism directly affects the endocrine and immune systems, or both."[2]

Permit me to offer a simpler explanation: If it's true that we are created "in the image of God," then we function most successfully when we share His opinion of the world.

Is Pessimism Genetic and Incurable?

Can pessimists ever learn to cheer up and to change their mental orientation? Or is pessimism genetic—you're just born with a frown instead of a smile?

You'll be happy to hear that psychologist Martin Seligman, of the University of Pennsylvania, concluded that pessimism is identifiable and can be changed so that some people might get therapy to alter their thinking about bad events and thereby improve their health.

Many other health professionals have come to agree with him. The current feeling is that optimism can be cultivated. Robert Thayer, a professor of psychology at California State University, Long Beach, in his book *The Origin of Everyday Moods,* says that most people erroneously think of optimism and pessimism as fixed traits. But he and his colleagues find that these feelings even in one and the same person tend to come and go. They are like moods that usually are associated with specific moments.

Thayer says optimism is closely related to our central energy state. "When we are feeling energetic and calm, we feel optimistic. Feeling tense and tired turns us into pessimists. This may even be tied into daily biological rhythms. Thayer found that many people tend to be more optimistic in the late morning than in the late afternoon when they are more likely to feel tired and tense.[3]

What Can You Do to "Have a Nice Day"?

Even those who seem to be predisposed to a bleak outlook on life can help themselves considerably in a number of ways:

■ Robert Thayer suggests that exercise can help tremendously. Even a brisk, ten-minute walk can change a person's whole outlook.

■ Dr. Robert Fox, attending psychiatrist at the Portland campus of St. Francis Care Behavioral Health, says helping others helps considerably to build optimism. It seems that loving your neighbor as yourself isn't just good for your neighbor; it's a powerful medicine for you as well. "Optimists," according to Fox, "discover that cooperation is better than competition."

■ Psychologist Michael Mercer, author of *Spontaneous Optimism: Proven Strategies for Health, Prosperity, and Happiness*, advises that the way to optimism is to concentrate on what you want in life, not on what you *don't* want. Optimists, he says, focus on solutions rather than problems. In other words, they switch from thinking, "I hate my boss," to "What can I do to build my career?"[4]

■ Mercer also stresses the importance of your environment. Spending time with constant complainers will influence your thinking. Having friends who enjoy life and laugh often will do wonders for your disposition.

■ Mercer suggests that you learn to use upbeat language. Never say you're tired. Just tell people you need to recharge your batteries.

■ Martin Seligman, director of clinical training at the University of Pennsylvania, Philadelphia, and author of *Learned Optimism*, stresses that we can choose how we think. Styles of thinking become habits. We can control our thoughts as we can our muscles. Pessimists tend to have hopeless thoughts. They tell themselves, "I'll never get it right," or "I always screw up," or worse, they stamp themselves with a negative label: "I must be stu-

pid." People have to learn to speak to themselves more
kindly, the way you would expect a loving friend to do.
If you acted like a jerk, don't give yourself that description in your own mind, but say, "Sometimes I'm not as
considerate as I'd like to be, but overall I know I'm a
kind person."[5]

■ Accept the wisdom of William James, who claimed that,
"The greatest discovery of my generation is that human
beings can alter their lives by altering their attitudes of
mind." Boost your mind by visualizing success or even
what a good cup of hot coffee would taste like if you're
freezing on the ski slope. Concentration camp survivors
often explain that their most important strategy for staying alive was imagining in their minds eating an entire
meal, from appetizer to dessert. They didn't get any cal-
ories but they did affirm their confidence that some day
their lives would be normal again.

■ Learn to look at people and think of their positive qualities rather than their faults. If the first thing you notice
about your date is that he's bald but don't even see his
beautiful smile and his kindly face, you're probably
doomed to a life of loneliness because nobody is good
enough for you.

The Bride Is So Beautiful

I think it will surely surprise you to hear that in Judaism there
is a moment when optimism is not only offered as a suggestion but attains the status of a required obligation—a reli-
giously binding law!

The source is the Talmud, a compilation of the most important discussions of scholars during the first 500 years of
our present-day calendar. Among the rabbis most often
quoted are Hillel and Shammai, the heads of the two major
academies of learning in the first century. Their debates cover

hundreds of subjects. There is one, however, that has special relevance for us.

The rabbis had agreed that it was the obligation of everyone present at a wedding to make the bride happy by complimenting her on her appearance. The phrase they suggest that every guest use is: "You are so very beautiful and virtuous."

The Talmud then presents us with an intriguing problem: What if the bride is *not* beautiful? What if, in fact, she is ugly as . . . well, sin? Are we still required to compliment her on her appearance? Or would we be violating the biblical commandment to speak only the truth?

Shammai views the ethical imperative of the book of Exodus, "From words of falsehood you shall keep far" (23:7), as binding and irrefutable. Hillel disagrees and demands that we offer the compliment even though we know it isn't true.

The rabbinic commentators struggle with the view of Hillel. How is it indeed possible for this great sage not only to condone but even to *command* what is normally considered sinful? The most accepted answer is that Hillel isn't asking us to lie. His ruling rests on our ability to find the beauty that is in every person, especially a bride on her wedding day, rather than to take notice of her more obvious faults.

Shammai says, "Tell it like it is." If she's homely, you aren't allowed to hide the truth from her. Hillel's view isn't only more compassionate, it is also prophetic. Tell a woman often enough that she is beautiful and the compliments will turn into reality.

Jewish law sides with the view of Hillel. Remember the old saying, "Beauty is in the eyes of the beholder"? That's not just a cliché. It's what should guide the comments of every wedding guest. *See* the beauty that is within every bride. *Believe* in the words you offer as praise. *Be an optimist*—and pray that your compliments, if they aren't yet true, will prove to be accurate in the near future.

The "Better" Students

Pygmalion in the Classroom, the classic study by R. Rosenthal and L. Jacobsen, dramatically illustrated the power that positive reinforcement and an optimistic perspective could have on students' performance.

An elementary school chosen for this experiment reported 20 percent of the children to their teachers as showing "unusual potential for intellectual growth." Actually, the names of these "highly gifted students" were drawn from a table of random numbers—the equivalent of picking numbers out of a hat!

Eight months later, these "special children" showed *significantly greater gains in IQ than all the others who had not been singled out for the teachers' attention.* The change of expectations regarding the intellectual performance of these supposedly superior students led to an actual and verifiable change in achievement by these randomly selected children. More striking still was the fact that these youngsters were subsequently described by professional interviewers—unaware of the study—as "more interesting, more motivated, showing greater intellectual curiosity and happier."[6]

Clearly, the preconceived attitudes of others not only define our abilities but also determine our destiny. And what the draw of a hat can do to us can surely be replicated by our own expectations. *We* can believe ourselves special—and by our own verdict make our assumption come true. *We* can consider ourselves gifted—and turn our self-image into reality. *We* can imagine ourselves blessed above 80 percent of the rest of the world—and discover that our optimistic conclusion becomes the real script of our life stories.

⌒ What You Want to Remember ⌒

- A pessimist is a person who is never happy unless he is miserable. That makes his attitude not just an opinion but a guarantee of a life that will bring him very little joy.

■ God is an optimist who proclaimed that the world is good. It's only right that we accept His view of the world—after all, He should know best because He is the one who created it. Pessimism is not only a disease of the soul, but a very significant indicator of future illness and shortened longevity.

■ Optimists don't have to be born, they can be created. Changing your mood is possible if you follow some simple prescriptions that will make you a happier person. The way you view people, from brides to students, profoundly affects the way they think of themselves. Positive words bring about positive results.

■ The most important step you have to take to deal with your financial loss is to make sure that your misfortune doesn't turn you into a pessimist. Remember that the key to your survival, both financial and physical, is not your position in life but your *dis*position.

■ Preconceived attitudes and expectations of others have been proven to affect our behavior and our abilities. What we think of ourselves can just as surely become self-fulfilling prophecies.

Notes

1. Toshihiko Maruta, Robert C. Colligan, Michael Malinchoc, and Kenneth P. Offord, "Optimists vs. Pessimists: Survival Rate Among Medical Patients Over a 30-Year Period," *Mayo Clinic Proceedings* 75 (February 2000), pp. 140–143.
2. Richard Schultz, Jamila Bookwala, Judith Knapp, Michael Scheier, and Gail Williamson, "Pessimism, Age and Cancer Mortality," *Journal of Psychology and Aging* 11, 2 (1996), pp. 304–309.

3. Robert Thayer, *The Origin of Everyday Moods* (New York: Oxford University Press, 1996).

4. Michael Mercer, *Spontaneous Optimism: Proven Strategies for Health* (Lake Zurich, Ill.: Castlegate Publishers, 1998).

5. Martin Seligman, *Learned Optimism* (New York: Random House, 1990).

6. R. Rosenthal and L. Jacobsen, *Pygmalion in the Classroom: Teacher Expectation and Pupils' Intellectual Development* (New York: Irvington, 1992).

CHAPTER 16

Are You Afraid of Success?

A champion is afraid of losing;
everyone else is afraid of winning.

—Billie Jean King

I know this is hard to believe.

In your own mind, you wanted nothing more than to be successful. You're sure that your goal was to be rich and famous. And yet, psychologists now confirm that there is a pervasive feeling among many people that they won't be able to cope with success and so, subconsciously, they sabotage their own expressed desire to win and manage to make sure that they fail.

Matina Horner, in a famous study published in *Psychology Today*, "A Bright Woman is Caught in a Double Bind," coined the phrase "fear of success" to describe the mechanism motivating people not to achieve their goals.

In Horner's research, based on 178 University of Michigan undergraduates, she wrote:

> A bright woman is caught in a double bind. In testing in other achievement-oriented situations, she worries not only about failure, but also about success. If she fails, she is not

living up to her own standards of performance; if she succeeds, she is not living up to societal expectations about the
female role.[1]

For far too many years, women looking for husbands were
advised not to appear too bright and not to win at any games
they played with men, for fear that their intelligence might
create too much of a threat to a potential husband.

Horner argues emphatically that women believed intellectual achievement and leadership roles, although considered
positive characteristics in men, were frowned upon by what
society deemed appropriate behavior for women.

Further research proved that this seemingly strange self-
defeating behavior was not restricted to women. In fact, it is
common not only in a large percentage of men, but it is particularly noticeable in a great number of the most successful
people.

Why should anyone fear success? Is it possible that the real
reason you keep making mistakes in the market is because,
deep down, you really want to buy high and sell low rather
than deal with all the consequences of having a huge fortune?
Dr. Martha Friedman, in her incisive book *Overcoming the
Fear of Success*, points out that Sigmund Freud, in his classic
work *Those Wrecked By Success*, already recognized this far-
reaching psychological problem when he wrote: "People oc-
casionally fall ill precisely because a deeply-rooted and long-
cherished wish has come to fulfillment. It seems then as
though they could not endure their bliss. Of the causative connection between this fulfillment and the falling ill, there can
be no question."[2]

By "falling ill," Freud explained that this included almost
all acts of self-defeating behavior, psychological as well as
physiological. Drugs, alcohol, addictions of all kinds, are ways
that people find to sabotage themselves. Even heart attacks,
from a psychological perspective, may be a person's deep-
rooted fulfillment of his lack of desire to go on living.

Why Should People Be Afraid of Success?

Do you know the dream almost everybody has very often? You're at a public function. It can be a social affair or even a religious gathering. Suddenly you realize that you are standing there stark naked. Everyone is staring at you. But there is nowhere to hide. They all see you "as you really are," with no covering to protect you.

The details of the dream may vary. Everyone has their own special place where they are afraid they will be seen as they truly are. The interpretation of the dream is obvious. We all fear that others will somehow find out our faults. We all know our own imperfections. Sometimes they are real. Sometimes they go back to our childhood when cruel parents, teachers, or friends kept telling us that we're stupid, we're lazy, we'll never amount to anything. We internalized the negative messages we so often received and in one part of our brain we adopted them as truth, because our authority figures and our parental idols said it was so.

We fear that some day we will lose our "covers." Clothes are meant not only to protect our modesty but to present a certain image of ourselves. Our dreams remind us that it's very possible for us to become dis-covered or un-covered.

Do not aspire too high, your inner self tells you. You will be noticed and then things will be expected of you that you are really incapable of achieving.

"I'm afraid that if I succeed," you tell yourself, "I will get in over my head, and then fail from an even higher, more embarrassing public level."

"If I succeed," you tell yourself again, "I will only bring out other people's envy, their anger and resentment, and even perhaps some kind of retaliation."

"If I amass a fortune and my father never made much of a living, I will be shaming his memory. How can I possibly be more than the father I want so much to admire?"

Martha Friedman sees this as the source of writer's block. This peculiar affliction seems to strike mainly those who have previously written a very highly praised work. The "block" comes from the fear that the author can't possibly duplicate the first effort. Critics will certainly see through him the next time, and he will be standing naked before the entire world. Better not to write at all than to face the possibility of being shamed in the presence of a very large audience.

Famous actors and actresses, rock stars, and musical legends, know in their heart of hearts that they don't deserve to be idolized. They, too, are afraid that their success must surely be the top of the mountain from which they will shortly fall off a cliff.

The fear of success is the fear of being found out. It's hard to accept more than what we ourselves realize we truly deserve.

The Advice to Jascha Heifetz

There is a remarkable letter that George Bernard Shaw once wrote to Jascha Heifetz after he heard him play. It reads:

> My dear Mr. Heifetz:
>
> My wife and I were overwhelmed by your concert. If you continue to play with such beauty, you will certainly die young. No one can play with such perfection without provoking the jealousy of the gods. I earnestly implore you to play something badly every night before going to bed.

What Shaw was advising was in fact the way primitive man responded to the fear of success. I know I don't deserve so much, so I will pay off the gods with sacrifices. I realize no one can have everything, so let me give up some of my animals, or perhaps even slaughter my son in order to appease the envy of the deities.

Although Jascha Heifetz didn't accept Shaw's recommendation, those who suffer from the "fear of success" syndrome make use of other strategies to prevent having to pay the price for their good fortune.

Gamblers don't really, deep down, believe they are going to beat the house. They know they're going to lose, and if they temporarily win they'll keep on playing. Even as they finally leave the casino with empty pockets, they have "won" what they were really seeking—losing in order to confirm their poor opinion of themselves.

The Fear of Exposure

Psychologists link the fear of success to the fear of exposure. The limelight is no place to be if there are secrets you have to hide.

Martha Friedman illustrates this powerfully with a story about Frederick, an American son of Polish-Jewish immigrants. Growing up in severe poverty, Frederick was ashamed of his family—his mother who worked from dawn to midnight in a small restaurant she established, and his two sisters, who had to leave school to become assistant cook and head waitress.

Frederick was pampered and encouraged to go to medical school, with the hard work of his family paying for his tuition. As Frederick progressed in his medical studies, he wanted to do his residency in orthopedics but felt that his being Jewish would stand in the way of his professional advancement. He decided that he had to cut his ties with his past, and so he stopped talking to his mother and sisters and changed his last name to one that he believed sounded "distinguished." He warned his mother and sisters never to get in touch with him for fear that contact might disclose the truth of his identity. Frederick went on to become a very successful orthopedic surgeon. But for the rest of his life he lived in constant trepidation of exposure.

He married an Episcopalian socialite. His mother, bewildered by this estrangement, took to bed and shortly thereafter died.

When, some years later, Frederick's older sister also passed away, he happened to be in the hospital taking care of one of his patients. He did not bother to go to his sister's room. The next morning he inexplicably could barely get out of bed. He suffered from terrible back pains, whose cause he could not identify. His condition deteriorated until he finally had to be hospitalized.

The orthopedic surgeon could no longer work because of his own back problem. His income was significantly reduced and he soon found himself on the verge of bankruptcy. His wife left him and he had no children. A short time later, Frederick was found on the floor of his office consulting room, dead by his own hand.

His obituary in one of the dailies began, "Society doctor Frederick Almond Chase III, born Samuel Rabinowitz . . ."

After years of living in dread that he would eventually be found out, his "secret" was now common knowledge. He spent his life fearing that success would lead to exposure. And he died with both his success forfeited and his secret unmasked.[3]

The Seven Sages

The Seven Sages of Greece were seven fabled wise men, who met at Delphi to dedicate their wise sayings to the god Apollo. Their names were Thales, Solon, Periander, Cleobulus, Chilon, Bias, and Pittacus. We're indebted to one of them for the two words that can help us change our lives: "Know thyself."

Self-awareness is the first step in dealing with self-sabotaging behavior. Knowing why we act as we do allows us to change our conduct. We can break our bad habits once we understand why we persist in holding on to them even though they are harmful. The extremely beautiful woman who can't understand why she became so fat might be shocked to learn that it was her subconscious way of discouraging the sexual advances that had become so intrusive when she was svelte. The businessman who kept failing would be able to break his string of "bad luck" if only he realized that he was subconsciously fulfilling his father's constant criticism of him as a "born loser."

There are times when we blame our failures on others, and we would do better to remember the words of attorney Louis Nizer: "When a man points a finger at someone else, he should remember that three of his fingers are pointing at himself." If you viewed the stock market the way a gambler considers craps or the roulette table, you may very well not have sold when you could have had a profit because you were secretly afraid of success!

⌐ What You Want to Remember ¬

- People don't only fear failure. There is a common syndrome identified by Matina Horner, psychologist and former president of Radcliff College, as the "fear of success."

- The fear of success, on the deepest level, is the fear of being found out, of people seeing us "without our clothing"—unmasked and naked. It has its roots in our own lack of self-esteem and self-worth.

- Fear of success can also have other subconscious sources, from the way we were treated as children to the way we fear falling from heights that we can't believe we have scaled (or feel we don't deserve).

- Fear of success is often related to fear of exposure. When not understood, it can lead not only to loss of money but even to loss of life.

- The injunction to "know thyself" has important bearing on the way we have to evaluate our stock market performance. A gambler's need for losing should never become the real reason for an investor's portfolio failures.

- Fear can torpedo our efforts in every area of our lives— our jobs, our financial security, our self-confidence. One of the most important stepping-stones to success is not to be afraid of it.

Notes

1. Matina Horner, "A Bright Woman Caught in a Double Bind," *Psychology Today* 3 (November 1969): 36–38, 62.
2. Martha Friedman, *Overcoming the Fear of Success* (New York: Putnam Publishing Group, 1980).
3. Ibid.

CHAPTER 17

Greed Is *Not* Good

*There is enough in this world for
everyone's need, but not enough
for everyone's greed.*

—Mahatma Gandhi

Why are so many otherwise smart people so inept when it comes to money?

Probably for the same reason that so many intelligent investors lose money in the market. Every Wall Street expert will tell you: "Bulls make money. Bears make money. Pigs get slaughtered."

When the valuations of stocks were way out of sight and the profit we could have made was almost obscene, the real question we have to ask ourselves is, why didn't we sell?

There's only one honest answer. It's because we were greedy. We wanted to squeeze out every last possible dollar from holdings that seemed to go nowhere but up. The god of greed never lets us sell before our stock reaches its ultimate record high. Only with the wisdom of hindsight do we realize that stocks never give us a signal exactly when they plan to fall.

Doctor Moola, almost certainly a pseudonym for a financial advisor with his own Web site (www.drmoola.com), is

132

right on the money when he offers this tip of how to succeed as a short-term trader:

> Most important is that you need to establish your sale parameters. This is where people usually go wrong. Recognize the fact that from time to time you should take your losses. If, after studying the stock you're interested in, you determine it can drop 15 percent below its market price on any given day, then you should establish your sale parameter 20 to 25 percent below your purchase price. Learn to take your losses right away. As soon as you hold on to try to get even, you are eventually doomed to seriously losing money.
>
> Establishing sale parameters on the downside will prevent losses from becoming so large that your entire portfolio performance will be seriously affected. But you also need to establish sale parameters when a holding is rising. *Do not try to squeeze out the last dollar of profit.* Put down a written goal that you would like to achieve. And don't waver when the stock reaches that point. If you're afraid it will continue to rise forever, with you now just watching, then at least include a partial sale as part of your goal.

Sounds pretty easy, doesn't it? So why don't people do it? Again, the one-word answer is greed.

In 1987, Michael Douglas won an Oscar for Best Actor in the movie *Wall Street*. In the film, Douglas played the role of Gordon Gekko, a fiendishly avaricious stock market speculator. To thunderous applause, in one of the climactic scenes of the film, Douglas alias Gekko tells his adoring audience: "There's a new law of evolution in corporate America. Greed is good."

It is a quote that has become an accepted motto in the years that followed. Many cultural analysts define the eighties and nineties as "decades of greed"—a time when only money counted and it didn't matter how you got it. It became socially acceptable to desire excessive amounts of material possessions. Greed became not only accepted, it was encouraged. Madonna, probably the most popular and influential entertainer in the world at the time, made a smash hit out of a song that emphasized, "I'm a material girl living in a material world." And I don't doubt that her choice of a so readily identifiable religious name, Madonna, was not by accident. She, in effect, became the leader of a new cult, the preacher for our contemporary moral perspective.

The new millennium, if anything, has not only accepted greed as good, but it encouraged it in ways that would have seemed utterly impossible years ago. The TV networks are grinding out instant millionaire shows that have become the saviors of ratings. ABC, for instance, was at the bottom of the heap of networks until Regis Philbin began minting millionaires on a regular basis. Even Chuck Woolery, a former game show host known for *The Dating Game* and *Wheel of Fortune*, was resurrected for a show named *Greed*. Contestants are asked to explain their "need for greed"—an obvious oxymoron that could make sense only to producers who live their own lives by this same creed.

There couldn't have been a more outlandish illustration of our idealization of greed than Fox TV's bizarre concept for a show called *Who Wants to Marry a Multi-Millionaire?* While the very notion seemed almost synonymous with legal prostitution, the reality is that thousands of contestants competed to marry a man they hadn't dated or even met just because he was a "multi-millionaire." Encouraging this gross display of greed were the more than 20 million people who actually tuned in to the premier show.

Perhaps the moral of the story became apparent in the aftermath of what happened with the "winner." Darva Conger was the "lucky one" to be chosen by Rick Rockwell. Darva married Rick for his money, and then said, "I feel very uncomfortable around him. He's just not a person that I would ordinarily have a friendly relationship with." Off on their honeymoon they went, to the Bahamas, with Darva insisting on separate cabins and separate rooms. The only thing she omitted from her demands was separate bank accounts. On national television, she revealed that she was highly embarrassed and angry by the public display of affection Rick showed her when he kissed her on the mouth just because he assumed she was soon to be his bride. Following her public denunciation of Rick's immodest behavior, Darva then went on to accept a *Playboy* proposal to appear as a centerfold!

Let's Talk Turkey

Some years ago, a popular ad read, "You don't have to be Jewish to love Levy's real Jewish rye bread." If I can just amend that a bit, you don't have to be religious to recognize that, contrary to Gekko's conclusion, greed is *not* good. Greed will always leave you dissatisfied because you'll never be able to get everything you desire. Greed never allows you to think you have enough; it always destroys you by making you strive ever harder for more. Perhaps most important of all, though, is that greed motivates us to make mistakes we would otherwise never be stupid enough to commit.

A friend of mine told me the secret of how he managed to come out ahead in the market. He said he always remembered the story of the farmer who set a trap for wild turkeys. The trap was a box about six feet square, with one side tilted up and supported by a pole. The farmer hid in the bushes and held on to a long cord tied to the pole. When he would jerk the cord, any turkeys that wandered under the box would be caught. To entice them to enter he left trails of corn leading to the trap.

One day, twelve turkeys came close to the trap and eleven of them stepped in. "In just a minute," the farmer thought to himself, "I'll have the other one too."

While he waited, three of the eleven in the trap walked out. That's when he wished he had been satisfied with the eleven. He made up his mind that as soon as one of the three went back in, he would pull the cord. Instead, five more walked out. That left only three turkeys inside. Surely, he thought, by waiting just a little bit longer he could count on at least two or three coming back to the corn he left inside the trap. As he was debating with himself on what to do, the remaining turkeys all left, leaving the trap empty.

My friend told me from that moment on he took to heart the moral of the story: The eleven turkeys the farmer could have had were just paper profits!

Bernard Baruch, the financial genius, summed it up best in one line: "I always made money by selling too soon."

Yes, Virginia, There Is an Alternative to Greed

CEOs and captains of industry were stunned by a story that made headlines all over the country. Aaron Feuerstein, the hero of this remarkable tale, realized that "Other CEOs feel I'm sort of a stupid guy who doesn't know what to do with his excess money." But Feuerstein not only intuitively knew the right thing that he had to do, but also believes that his example will eventually become accepted as a model for success in the twenty-first century.

Feuerstein is the owner of Malden Mills, a business founded by his grandfather in 1906. On December 11, 1995, while Aaron Feuerstein was celebrating his seventieth birthday in a Boston restaurant, an explosion almost completely destroyed his textile factory. The sane and standard business decision would have been to collect the insurance and to close the business. Feuerstein knew, however, that if he closed his factory, which was in an economically depressed region of old mill towns north of Boston, 3,100 high-paying manufacturing jobs would disappear.

Feuerstein, a devout Jew, said that everything about his upbringing and his fifty-year history in the local business told him to rebuild. "It was the right thing to do and there is a moral imperative to do it irrespective of the consequences." Smoke was still rising from the rubble when Feuerstein prepared to speak to his workers at a Lawrence high school gym.

"We were ready to hear that it was over," recalls Paul Coorey, the union local president. Surely, he thought, the owner would take the $300 million in insurance money and then relocate to a place where labor was cheaper. In all honesty, Coorey thought, Feuerstein would be stupid not to do exactly that.

Instead, here's what happened: Feuerstein took the microphone and started making promises, promises that would cost him $1.5 million in payroll every week. He committed himself not only to rebuilding the plant, but to pay every worker's December wages as well as a $275 Christmas bonus.

The workers who came expecting to be laid off cried like babies. They offered prayers of thanks and promised their everlasting loyalty. As for Feuerstein, Peter Jennings named him Person of the Week, and Tom Brokaw referred to him as "a saint for the nineties" and "the best boss in America." President Clinton invited him to be a guest of honor at his State of the Union Address.

Greed lost out to goodness. What's even more important is that Aaron Feuerstein's model of corporate compassion has had a trickle-down effect. "He's still pretty lonely, but the idea has appeal," said Michael Useem, professor of management at the University of Pennsylvania's Wharton School. "The thinking is: Employees can be seen as an ultimate competitive advantage. If you treat them well, they'll pay you back in really hard work later on." Remarkably enough, in a study by Massachusetts Institute of Technology professor Paul Osterman, he found that between a quarter and a third of U.S. companies are taking steps to convert to a model like Feuerstein's.[1] Who knows? Maybe the time will come when sound business judgment will dictate that Michael Douglas was wrong and Aaron Feuerstein was right!

Why the Pig Is So Hated

There is an ancient legend that records a conversation between a pig and a cow. The pig, deeply perplexed, asks his fellow creature to explain why people have such a totally different relationship to the two of them. "I give mankind so many things. From my hide, they make pigskin and enjoy all kinds of clothing. From the various parts of my body they derive edible pleasure. Pigs feet, pigs knuckles, spareribs, hog jowl, chitterlings, as well as bacon, one of the staples of their morning breakfast. Yet look at how they treat me. My very name is associated with gluttony and filth and is used as a curse. My reputation is so soiled that even the Bible considers me a forbidden animal. You, however, are so much more respected. You conjure up an image of contentment. People pamper you, praise you, and love you. Yet all you do for them is give them some milk. Why is your contribution so much more appreciated?"

The cow hesitated for but a moment and then responded with great insight: "It is true that you may give more, but my charitableness carries greater weight because I give when I am still alive."

Greedy people, it's been said, give until it hurts—and they have an extremely low threshold of pain. A greedy person doesn't understand the great discovery of Peyton March that, "There is a law of nature that the three things we crave most in life—happiness, freedom, and peace of mind—are always attained by giving them to someone else." Greed makes people hold on to everything they have until they leave this world and discover they can't take it with them. What they could not force themselves to give away while alive finds its way into the hands of lawyers and taxes as well as ungrateful heirs who remember how they were ignored during the deceased's lifetime. The memories that a miser leaves behind are all disagreeable, which is why his reputation forever remains that of a pig.

The Geography of Greed

According to the Bible, as well as many major religions, God has a special affinity for the land of Israel. For centuries, people of many faiths have referred to it as "the Holy Land." In Jewish tradition, the land is linked to God even by its geography, which offers us spiritual lessons applicable to our own lives.

In the north of Israel, there is a sparkling river. The Jordan is the source of much-needed water in an arid climate. Fish abound there and serve as a delectable food supply. It is beautiful to behold and commonly acknowledged as a source of life.

That very same river flows south into another sea. From these waters, neither man nor beast will drink. It is foul smelling and forbidding.

What could possibly account for the difference between these two waters? The Sea of Galilee receives the waters of the Jordan but does not greedily retain them. For every drop that it gets, it gives another. The sea into which it flows, however, has a different mode of behavior. Every drop that it gets, it keeps. So while the Sea of Galilee generously gives and lives, its terminus that only knows how to hold on to what it has is called the Dead Sea.

The seas of Israel serve as symbols of people. Those who give, live. "Ninety percent of all mental illness that comes before me could have been prevented, or cured, by ordinary kindness," claims William McGrath, professor at National University. As Erich Fromm, the famous psychiatrist, put it, "Not he who has much is rich, but he who gives much."

Ironic, isn't it, that after all is said and done, it is the greedy who are really needy!

⟶ What You Want to Remember ⟶

■ Greed is the most common mistake people make, both in the stock market as well as in life.

■ Contemporary culture continues to try to force us to believe that, "Greed is good." In fact, greed causes us to make incredibly stupid decisions, be it in holding on to stocks that should be sold or in marrying someone just because he is a multimillionaire.

- There is a good reason why bulls and bears can make money but pigs will always get slaughtered.

- Truly successful businessmen don't have to be paradigms of greed. Aaron Feuerstein proved how the philosophy of treating employees like family can pay dividends in the long run while it still allows owners to remain true to their ethical and moral values. And Ace Greenberg is known to say, "The more I give, the more I earn."

- In the words of nineteenth-century English author and clergyman Charles Caleb Colton, "Posthumous charities are the very essence of selfishness when bequeathed by those who, even alive, would part with nothing."

- The Sea of Galilee and the Dead Sea pointedly symbolize the difference between those who practice giving and those who live by the creed of greed.

Note

1. Paul Osterman, *Securing Prosperity: The American Labor Market: How It Has Changed and What to Do About It* (Princeton, N.J.: Princeton University Press, 1999).

CHAPTER 18

Go to a Funeral

Who thinks of death improves himself.

> —Bahya Ibn Pakuda,
> eleventh-century Spanish
> rabbi and philosopher

Don't worry. In spite of the title, this chapter won't be morbid. As a matter of fact, if the economy still has you feeling down, the advice I am going to give you now should help considerably.

Actually, the idea isn't my own. It comes from the Bible, in the Book of Ecclesiastes. The author writes: "It is better to go to the house of mourning than to go to the house of feasting; for that is the end of all men, and the living will take it to heart" (Ecclesiastes 7:2).

What Solomon meant is beautifully expressed in a well-known poem by Robert Browning Hamilton:

I walked a mile with Pleasure
She chattered all the way
But left me none the wiser
For all she had to say.

I walked a mile with Sorrow
And ne'er a word said she

141

But oh the things I learned from her
When Sorrow walked with me.[1]

A house of feasting allows us to forget. A house of mourning forces us to remember. The first may give us pleasure, but the second grants us meaning. Contact with death and attendance at a funeral permit us to view our own lives from a different perspective. Death takes the sick but it also teaches the living.

The Talmud, the classic Jewish work of law and lore, tells the story of a sage who taught his students, "Repent one day before your death." His pupils did not understand, and one of them dared to ask how it was possible, since no man knows the time of his death?

"Exactly," replied the rabbi. "That is why every person ought to treat each day as if it were to be his last."

Far from being frightening, the recognition of the imminence and the inevitability of death allows us to focus on what is really important in the limited time we are granted the blessing of life.

In the holy city of Jerusalem, there is a synagogue built by immigrants from Persia, who to this day maintain a remarkable custom. Built into a wall of their house of worship there is a coffin clearly visible to all those present. When I attended services there, I asked for an explanation of this unusual architectural addition. The rabbi explained that it was to fulfill the words of the Talmudic sage who asks us always to think of the possibility that this might be the last day of our earthly existence.

The psychologist and anthropologist, Henry Abramovitch, in his essay "Death," makes the point that far from being depressing, the constant awareness of death "brings us all the more into life and its divinely conceived moral dimension."[2] Simply put, we learn how to live when we take to heart that we are someday going to die.

Do It Now–Tomorrow May Be Too Late

If you're still obsessed about money—making and losing it—remember what Paul Tsongas, the former senator from Massachusetts, said upon retiring in order to spend more time with his family, "I don't know anyone who on his deathbed expressed the wish that he had spent more time at the office."

In the presence of death we gain proper priorities. Go to a funeral and realize how petty are your tears for a thousand-point drop in the Dow compared to the grief of a wailing widow, of a dazed and lonely widower, of parents who must evermore bear the burden of a child whose growth to maturity they will never see, or of children who have just lost one or both of their parents.

Socrates said it this way: "If all the misfortunes of mankind were cast into a public stock, in order to be equally distributed among the whole species, those who now think themselves the most unhappy would prefer the share they are already possessed of, before that which would fall to them by such a division."

Going to a funeral reminds us of the difference between troubles and tragedy.

Before You Know It . . .

Go to a funeral . . . and reflect upon how fleeting is life.

Billy Crystal's character, in the 1991 movie *City Slickers*, powerfully captured this truth in a scene that was as philosophical as it was funny. Asked to address the kids in his child's class, he said:

> Value this time in your life, kids. It goes by so fast. When you're a teenager, you think you can do anything, and you do. Your twenties are a blur. Thirties—you raise a family, you make a little money, you think to yourself, "What happened to my twenties?" Forties—you grow a little potbelly, you grow another chin. The music starts to get too loud. One of your old girlfriends from high school becomes a

grandmother. Fifties—you have minor surgery. You call it a "procedure" but it's surgery. Sixties—you have major surgery. The music is still loud but it doesn't matter because you can't hear it anyway. Seventies—you and the wife retire to Fort Lauderdale. You start eating dinner at two o'clock in the afternoon. You have lunch around ten. Breakfast the night before. Spend most of your time wandering around malls looking for the urinal and muttering, "How come the kids don't call? How come the kids don't call?"

Who can argue with this short synopsis of life? Billy has made it Crystal-clear that, in the words of the Bible, "our days on the earth are as a shadow" (I Chronicles, 29:15). We only have our youth for a little while. Our middle years rush by like a whirlwind. We spend our old age making appointments with doctors. Living life to the fullest while we have it, enjoying our children and grandchildren, finding time for our families and friends ought to be our major preoccupations. Instead, we spend the days of our lives trying to make money when we're young and trying to buy youth when we're old.

The Tragedy of "Every Man"

There is a famous story told by the Russian novelist, Leo Niko-laevich Tolstoy, a tale that resonates with the tragedy of human behavior:

> *A nobleman, goes the story, wished to reward one of his feudal serfs. He told him that he would bestow great blessing upon him. He would give him the gift of a large piece of land, the exact size of which would be determined by the serf himself.*
>
> *Next morning he would grant him the opportunity to arise early. From sunrise to sunset he might walk and encircle a parcel of land. Whatever he would succeed in walking round would be his. There would be only one condition: the serf*

must return exactly to the starting point or he would forfeit everything.

How grateful the serf was for this once-in-a-lifetime opportunity! His plan to fulfill the nobleman's condition was simple. He would walk in one direction until the sun would be directly overhead. Then, knowing it was noon and obviously half his time had elapsed, he would begin his return journey. In that way he could be certain to be back at the starting point by sunset. That would give him a great parcel of land. That would allow him and his family to be rich beyond his wildest dreams.

And so he set off on his journey, his road to personal fulfillment and riches. He quickened his pace as the sun continued its ascent. Every additional step meant additional land, all his rushing would be rewarded with more riches. When noon arrived, he could not bear the thought that this would mark the end of his opportunity for acquiring land. If he were to go a little further and hasten his steps on the return journey; if he would extend the first part of his walk, encircling just a little bit more, and then run the entire way to return to the starting point in order to meet the condition, why then he might not be just a wealthy man, but a very, very, rich man. He might have enough not only for his children and grandchildren, but even for countless generations to come.

And so he walked to acquire new land for half an hour, an hour, two hours beyond noon. Panic overtook him as he realized how far he had gone and how great the distance in order to make it to the point from which he started his journey. Jogging, running, racing—he must make it back or else all of his efforts would prove futile. It was on the return

*journey that people stopped him to ask him for different
things. One needed a favor desperately. It was a matter of life
and death. "Tomorrow," he shouted out, "tomorrow I will
help you. Today I do not have the time." Another was his
own child who was hurt and begged, "Father, father, please
heal my wound, comfort me with words. I need you, Daddy."
"Tomorrow, my child, tomorrow. Tomorrow I'll have time to
spend with you. Tomorrow I will have time to play with you.
Tomorrow, not today. Don't you see how busy I am? And I'm
doing it all just for you."*

*His wife, too, tried to speak to him in the midst of his busy
race. "Just one word, my husband. Just one word. I cannot
solve this problem myself. I need to speak with you or I will
go mad. I need you to talk to me the way you did when we
were courting, when you were my pillar of strength, when
you were my everything, when I could turn to you no matter
what I needed." "Tomorrow," said the husband to his wife,
"tomorrow, tomorrow I will have all the time you need." And
he rushed right past her.*

*The race was now between the sun on the horizon and his
frantic footsteps to the starting point. So far had he misjudged
his ability to retrace the ground he had covered that it now
seemed almost impossible for him to complete his journey.
Faster, faster, and faster still. Now he had to race with
superhuman effort. His heart beat faster, his legs felt as if they
would cave in beneath him.*

*The sun had almost disappeared. The master was in the
distance waiting at the prearranged spot. With one final
lunge, the serf leaped to the required spot at almost the very
last second, legally fulfilling the condition set upon him. He
smiled the smile of the victor. The smile froze on his face in a
death mask as his soul departed from him.*

"Take this peasant and bury him in a plot six feet long, two feet wide," commanded the master. "Let him lie there. Let the land be his. That is all the ground he really ever needed."

We race through life and we ignore those who are truly important to us. For each of them we have an answer: Tomorrow. Tomorrow and we shall help you. Tomorrow and we shall be with you. Tomorrow and we shall have time for everything. Today I must make my fortune. Today I must still hurry. Yet tomorrow never comes as we live out our days, rushing to possess those things that will allow us a comfortable future—a future we forfeit in the present as we constantly occupy ourselves with foolish pursuits that prevent us from ever engaging in the truly meaningful tasks of life.

Go to a funeral and observe how much people leave undone for a never-to-appear tomorrow in order to pursue the fortune they will never live to spend. Rabbi Andrew Sachs, I believe, summed it up best: "Death is more universal than life. Everyone dies, but not everyone lives."

You Think *You've* Got Problems?

There's one last reason why I recommend that you go to a funeral in order to feel better about your financial problems. Prove to yourself that adversity is shared by everyone and is the price we pay for our presence on earth. Observe the pain of true mourning and bless God that your affliction at present is limited to loss of money.

The one experience that is common to all mankind is sorrow. A familiar story illustrates its universality. A patient came to a physician in the City of Naples. He complained of melancholia. He could not rid himself of a deep feeling of depression. The physician said, "I advise you to visit the theater where the incomparable Carlini is appearing. This great comedian daily convulses large crowds with laughter. By all means, go to see Carlini. His performance will undoubtedly drive away your depression."

At these words, the patient burst into tears and sobbed uncontrollably. "But doctor," he responded, "you don't understand. I *am* Carlini!"

In the presence of death, you remind yourself that you were not singled out for sadness. To be human is to have an unavoidable date with death. To be wise is to distinguish between what is transient and what is everlasting, what is impermanent and what would make your memory immortal.

The Fist and the Open Hand

The rabbis of the Talmud note a fascinating difference demonstrated by our fingers when we are born and when we die. An infant comes out of the womb with fists clenched. A dying person flings his hands open.

For the sages of old, this could not be viewed merely as coincidence. There is profound symbolism in these two contrary motions. The newborn clenches his fist as if to say, "I plan to conquer the world. Everything will be in my hands. All earthly possessions are in my grasp."

Death brings with it the final revelation: We thrust open our hands as if to declare, "You see, we take nothing with us to the grave."

"You can't take it with you" isn't just a proverb. It's a concept physically expressed at the two boundaries of life. Understanding it grants us the greatest gift of all: to grasp the true purpose of life. Gold isn't as important as God. Acquiring money isn't as meaningful as earning a good name that will remain as a perpetual monument for your achievements.

⌐ What You Want to Remember ⌐

- Death not only takes, but it also teaches. Awareness of our inevitable end forces us to focus on living life in an authentic fashion.

■ Attending a funeral makes us sensitive to the suffering of others, which often makes our own problems pale in comparison.

■ Funerals remind us of the fleeting nature of life. With the unalterable fact that our days are limited in number, we must learn to prioritize so that our time is used in a manner consistent with our values.

■ In our race of life, it is the greatest foolishness to defer what is truly important to a tomorrow that will never arrive, for the sake of material possessions that we will never have the opportunity to use.

■ Gold doesn't accompany us to the grave but, in the words of the Bible, "A good name is better than precious ointment" (Ecclesiastes 7:1) and grants its bearer immortality.

Notes

1. Robert Browning Hamilton, "Along the Road."
2. Henry Abramovitch, "Death," in *Contemporary Jewish Religious Thought*, Arthur A. Cohen, editor (New York: Touchstone Books, April 1988).

CHAPTER 19

Why the Bible Is Better than Buffett

*A thorough knowledge of the Bible is worth
more than a college education.*

—Theodore Roosevelt

Warren Buffett is widely considered America's greatest investor. He is this country's second richest man, with a fortune
valued at over $15 billion. Buffett made his money through
Berkshire Hathaway, a $50-billion holding company for invest-
ments he personally selected. The phenomenal success of
Berkshire Hathaway can be seen from its share price. It was
$19 in 1964, and is around $70,000 today. The average return
has been almost 25 percent per annum, with no year of losses.
No wonder he is known as "The Sage of Omaha."

Obviously, Buffett knows his business. I applaud his bril-
liance as well as his accomplishments. His investment philosophy is clearly based on sound principles.

But we aren't Buffett. We—that's you, the reader, and I—
made major mistakes in how we handled our finances. What
we certainly don't want to do is to repeat our errors. We need
good advice to help us better manage our money.

It may seem strange, at first glance, for me to tell you that
some of the very best fiscal guidance ever given, as relevant

today as when it was first written, is found in the Bible. As you'll see in this chapter, American patriot and Revolutionary War hero Patrick Henry had good reason to write, "There is a book worth all the other books that were ever printed. It is called the Bible."

My purpose in this book, as its subtitle makes clear, is spiritual therapy. So far I've tried to comfort and console, as well as to put the meaning of your loss into perspective. It's time for some more specific therapy to make sure you've finally learned the right lessons from your misfortune and won't ever let it happen to you again. And for these suggestions we're going to go to the Book of Books written by God, who is even smarter than Buffett.

Yes, God, who stresses the spiritual over the material, still cares about money. He inserted crucial ideas about its acquisition and its management in His book intended to teach us how to conduct ourselves in every area of our lives. And the bonus, believe it or not, is that with God you can do even better than with Berkshire Hathaway.

Let's pick just a few stories and verses from Scripture to reflect upon concepts that could have saved us a fortune in the past and can still protect us in the future:

> And Joseph said unto Pharaoh: The dream of Pharaoh is one; what God is about to do He has declared unto Pharaoh. The seven good cows are seven years and the seven good stalks are seven years. The dream is one. And the seven lean and ill-favored cows that came up after them are seven years, and also the seven empty stalks blasted with the east wind, they shall be seven years of famine . . . behold, there comes seven years of plenty throughout all the land of Egypt. And there shall arise after them seven years of famine, and all the plenty shall be forgotten in the land of Egypt (*Genesis 41:25–30*).

Joseph taught Pharaoh a startling new idea that had previously never been recognized. There is an economic cycle that constantly repeats itself, taking us from prosperity to poverty, only to replicate the pattern over and over again. The gist of Joseph's advice, which saved Egypt's economy and allowed it to become a world power, was simple: Prepare in the good times for the bad times that will surely follow.

Fast forward to 1929. While the poor had sunk their savings into a market they were assured could only go up, American statistician, business forecaster, and author Roger Babson warned in September of that year: "Fair weather cannot always continue. The economic cycle is in progress today, as it was in the past. The Federal Reserve System has put the banks in a strong position, but it has not changed human nature. More people are borrowing and speculating today more than ever in our history. Sooner or later a crash is coming and it may be terrific."

It isn't true that people had no advance warning for the Crash of '29. James Dale Davidson and Sir William Rees-Mogg, in their book about this crisis, *Blood in the Streets*, quote Paul Clay of Moody's Investor Service, who on December 28, 1928, spoke about that time's major "injurious financial fallacies." Clay said, "First among these fallacies is the New Era delusion as typified by the famous dictum, 'This is a new era. Statistics of the past don't count.' Every period of great prosperity is considered to be a new era and so much better fortified to give promise of permanence."[1]

Sound familiar? Before the most recent crash of 2000, newspapers and magazines overflowed with stories about the "new paradigm"—the notion that thanks to increased global competition and technological advances, inflation and the business cycle are dead. The advanced economies, in other words, could look forward to uninterrupted years of strong growth and low inflation, and the exuberance of equity prices around the world was thereby justified.

In March 1999, Merrill Lynch equity strategist Hugh Dougherty fearlessly pointed out that the markets were unbelievably strong and there was no room for concern: "We are genuinely in uncharted territory—there are no chart points or critical levels we can refer to." In other words, forget the past and the theory of economic cycles. Joseph was wrong. The cows and the stalks of Pharaoh's dream had been replaced by bulls. As the *Economist* pointed out on July 18, 1998: "The key to Wall Street's continuing miracles, bulls have started arguing, is the new courage of small investors. The suggestion is the rules that they have followed in the past no longer apply. Having overcome a previously irrational fear of the risks of equities, they are pouring into them."

Too bad everyone forgot yet another all-important piece of Biblical advice:

> *The thing that has been, it is that which shall be; and that which is done is that which shall be done; and there is nothing new under the sun (Ecclesiastes 1:9).*

What is even more incredible, some economists pointed out, is that the *duration* of financial cycles also correlates to biblical laws:

> *At the end of every seven years, you shall grant a release of debts. And this is the form of the release: Every creditor who has lent anything to his neighbor shall release it (Deuteronomy 15:1–2).*

> *And you shall count . . . seven times seven years . . . forty-nine years. Then you shall cause the trumpet of the Jubilee to sound on the tenth day of the seventh month; on the Day of Atonement (Yom Kippur), you shall make the trumpet to sound throughout all your land. For the fiftieth year shall be holy, a time to proclaim liberty throughout the land to all enslaved debtors and a time for canceling of all public and private debts. It shall be a year when all the family estates*

sold to others shall be returned to the original owners for their heirs (Leviticus 25:8–10).

Just as Joseph spoke of seven good years followed by seven lean years, economic history seems to indicate a general pattern of recessions every seven to eight years with a major depression approximately every fifty years. The cancellation of short-term debt after seven years and the return of land every fifty years may perhaps be the Bible's way of helping all those hurt by the consequences of inevitable economic cycles.

Business journalist Ross Gittins gives the dates of the recessions in Australia as a perfect illustration of the seven-year intervals: 1974–1975, 1982–1983, 1990–1991. Although there is certainly wide latitude possible for these time periods, due to a host of variables in every country, the boom-to-bust sequence described in the Bible has had ample confirmation throughout history.

In 1999, Warren Buffett linked Joseph's prediction to Pharaoh with the performance of the Dow Jones *toward the close of the twentieth century*: "Thirty-five years ago on December 31, 1964 an almost Biblical kind of symmetry, in the sense of lean years and fat years, began to happen to the stock market. At the beginning of this period the Dow Jones Industrial Average was at 874.12. Seventeen years later, on December 31, 1981, the Dow was at 875.24. This miniscule gain in price of the 30 stocks in this index took place during a period when the American economy, measured by the Gross Domestic Product (GDP) almost quadrupled, rising by 371 percent. Or if we look at another measure of economic growth, the profits earned by the Fortune 500 (a changing mix of large companies) more than sextupled. All this happened while the Dow Jones went exactly nowhere."[2]

James Dale Davidson and Sir William Rees-Mogg, financial advisors and authors of *Blood in the Streets*, are intrigued by yet another aspect of timing apparent in economic cycles. They write:

Even more mysterious is the strange tendency for major crashes to occur in the autumn, especially in October. For example, September 18, 1873; October 29, 1929; October 6, 1932; October 18, 1937; October 19, 1987; and October 13, 1989. Each of these dramatic results, among the largest drops ever recorded, occurred in the fall. The old view would be to argue that this is only coincidence, which of course is possible. Most likely some factor we do not now understand increases the vulnerability to sell-offs in the fall.[3]

What could there possibly be in that time period that from a divine perspective makes it so susceptible to terrible downfalls? Allow me to suggest a possible answer: On the Jewish calendar, *these dates always coincide with the period of the High Holy Days, biblically designated as the time of Heavenly Judgment!*

> *For the Lord your God blesses you as He promised you: And you shall lend unto many nations, but you shall not borrow; and you shall reign over many nations, but they shall not reign over you (Deuteronomy 15:6).*

David Mackie, an economist at J. P. Morgan, points out that American companies today have "a negative savings ratio," because they have been borrowing so much to invest. Corporate debt today represents 46 percent of the nation's gross domestic product, the highest level ever in history.

The Economist, on March 20, 1999, recorded that "new data from the Fed shows that America's financial sector borrowed a record $1.1 trillion last year, up from $653 billion in 1997." On April 22, 2000, as the effects of this huge borrowing began to be seen in the stock market averages, *The Economist* added that the heavy borrowing "might be fine if the debt had been used mainly to finance investments that would boost future productivity and profits. But about half of all corporate borrowing over the past two years has been used to buy back shares, which has helped prop up the stock market."

Prophetically, and confirming the biblical mandate that nations will be blessed provided that "you shall not borrow," *The Economist* of January 2, 1999, wrote: "Running up debts to finance investment may make sense in conditions of rapid economic growth. But, when growth slows and profitability tumbles, heavy indebtedness will force companies to make ferocious cuts in capital spending. This could be severe enough to push the American economy into a deep recession. A similar thing happened in Japan, that other 'miracle' economy, in the early 1990s. Companies had been borrowing and investing as though the economy would grow forever. Its economy is still paying the price. Japan's problems have mired Asia in recession. If America's economy went down the plug hole, the rest of the world will probably follow suit."

The borrower is servant to the lender *(Proverbs 22:7).*

How's that for the most pungent biblical argument against going on margin?

Somehow it makes sense to many Americans (as it does to our government) that it's okay to borrow money you have no idea how you're going to repay. More, it's perfectly sane to invest money you don't really have in stocks that may go up or down—and if they go down, you get sold out and lose everything you had!

Let's do one more comparison between the 1920s and today. One of the hallmarks of the prosperity of the 1920s was the easy condition of consumer credit markets. "Millions of families," according to Harold Evans in *The American Century*, "were in debt for the first time, buying on the installment plan. Personal debt more than doubled, from $3.1 billion in 1921 to $6.9 billion in 1929. The incipient recession in 1929 had already made consumers think twice about taking on more debt, because suddenly incomes began to look less assured. In 1930, even before earnings declined, and while government spending and investments were still rising, consumer spending suffered a spectacular ten percent fall."[4]

Now let's reflect on what's happening today. Consumer spending has risen almost twice as fast as income over the past few years, as capital gains have encouraged consumers to run down past savings and to expand their borrowings. Consumer installment debt outstanding at the beginning of the new millennium was $1.437 trillion. Consumer borrowing has soared from $770 billion in 1992. The average U.S. household, according to Gregory Zuckerman, staff reporter for *The Wall Street Journal*, now has thirteen credit or charge cards, and carries $7,500 in credit card balances, up from $3,000 in 1990. Nowadays, Zuckerman proves, even a poor credit history doesn't preclude someone from being deluged with offers of credit.[5] (A friend of mine received a letter addressed to his dog assuring him that because of his outstanding credit rating, they would be very pleased to send him a $5,000-limit credit card!) The total American household debt has jumped from 85 percent of personal income in 1992 to 103 percent last year. Clearly, as *The Economist* points out, "Spending cannot exceed income forever. The share-price gains which have been driving growth must, eventually, come to an end."

Margin debt tripled over the past five years preceding the market's bust. Borrowing by clients of New York Stock Exchange member firms rose 5 percent to a record $278.5 billion in April 2000. It had never been higher as a percentage of the market, according to investment research firm TrimTabs.com. "When this happens, it signals a speculative excess and historically a market top," said Charles Biderman, president of Trim-Tabs.com. At the height of the bull market in 2000, margin debt equaled 1.54 percent of the market value of U.S. companies, the largest ever. It stood at 1.37 percent in September of 1987, a month before the crash that sent the Dow Jones industrial average down 23 percent in one day.

That's probably why William Shakespeare expanded on

the biblical admonition and said: "Neither a borrower, nor a lender be." At the very least, remember that the first commandment records that God took us *out* of slavery. If the Book of Proverbs is right and "The borrower is servant to the lender," why voluntarily choose to turn yourself into a slave?

You shall not follow a multitude to do wrong (Exodus 23:2).

Did you ever hear of the "Tulip Bulb Mania" that spread through The Netherlands in the early 1600s? The flowers were imported from Turkey. As demand started to soar, prices were pushed to amazing levels, and the tulip-crazed Dutch saw the tulips as a get-rich-quick sure thing. In a panic, people reportedly mortgaged their homes and businesses to buy tulips. At the peak of the mania, a single tulip bulb sold for the equivalent of $150,000 or $1.5 million, depending on which historian you believe.

How was that possible? Scottish journalist Charles MacKay observed that, "Men think in herds; it will be seen that they go mad in herds, while they only recover their senses slowly, and one by one."

In the past few years we didn't call them tulip bulbs. Instead they were known as Internet start-ups and dot-com companies. Historically, according to the Center for Economic and Policy Research in Washington, D.C., stocks have been valued at about fourteen times earnings over the last seventy-five years. In 1929, some stocks were selling at fifty times earnings. As one expert put it, the markets were discounting not merely the future but the hereafter as well. At the height of the Internet mania, at the close of the millennium, earnings were simply irrelevant. The more a company spent, the higher its stock soared. "Follow the majority to do wrong" became almost a national ideal.

The way of a fool is right in his own eyes (Proverbs 12:15).

As a dog returns to his vomit, so a fool returns to his folly (Proverbs 26:11).

There's only one explanation for what happened to cause the crash. Too many people really believed the Greater Fool theory. I know what I'm buying is overpriced. But who cares? There'll always be somebody else greedy enough to buy it from me at a higher price. And, lo and behold, there finally came a day when there no longer was a "greater fool."

You shall not take a bribe because a bribe blinds the eyes of the wise and perverts the words of the righteous (Deuteronomy 16:19).

Where were all the experts who should have warned you? Why is "sell" the one word that major institutions as well as stockbrokers and analysts almost never use? According to Charles Hill, director of research at Thomson Financial/First Call (as quoted in *The New York Times* of July 1, 2001), just 1 percent of all analyst stock ratings are "sell," while nearly half are "buy." Even worse, studies by the investment research firm of Multex.com show that *at the height of the market in the Spring of 2000, only one-fifth of 1 percent (.002%) of all stock recommendations were "sells."* The worst rating most analysts will ever give a stock is "hold."

Do you know why? Because all of these people make a living from recommending stocks. The largest investment houses have corporations as major clients, who would be incensed if the people they're paying to make deals came out with negative reports.

Are they consciously trying to mislead you? Not necessarily. But remember the words of the Bible: *Bribes make even the wise turn blind.* Self-interest almost always beats honesty. Analysts are *interested* in maintaining good relations with their clients; they are *afraid* that if they downgrade a company, they will get cut out of the information loop; they are *careful* not to change ratings after so many money managers who trusted them have invested; and, like all of us, they *want to believe* that their first analysis was correct.

That's why, if those who advise us what to do with our money were to repeat the former mayor of New York's famous question, "How am I doing?"—the reply would have to be worse than what almost anyone would have answered Ed Koch. How bad were the recommendations we were given by the "experts"? Since January 1997, 16 of the 19 largest U.S. brokerages have issued money-losing stock advice, according to investment research firm Investars.com. Even the bank with the best overall rating—Credit Suisse First Boston—had returns below 7 percent for traders who precisely followed its advice. None of the top-rated investment banks achieved positive returns on hardware, software, or communications technology stocks—the very industries they touted as the most promising and rewarding in both the short and long term.

How can we explain this incredibly horrible performance? Let's stress once again that in all certainty it's not a conscious effort to defraud clients. It's just a Biblical warning come true. Bribes in any form serve as blinders and prevent even experts from seeing!

The Talmud records the story of a judge who while walking up to the bench was helped up the stairs. When the judge learned that the man who assisted him was one of the litigants about to be tried, he excused himself by saying, "I can no longer be impartial. I have been bribed by his act of kindness."

That was a judge who was sworn to decide fairly. Nevertheless, he felt that he could no longer see the matter before him with total objectivity. Just imagine, then, how objective your boiler room recommendations and Internet message board tips can be!

In a stern speech, Laura Unger, then acting chairwoman of the Securities and Exchange Commission, warned Wall Street firms to resolve the "blatant" conflicts that surround the business of bringing shares to the public and then recommending them to investors. After Eliot Spitzer, New York's Attorney General, launched an investigation of Merrill Lynch for "possible willful promotion by Merrill's stock analysts of shares they privately considered to be duds" (subpoenaed inter-office e-mails included references to *recommended* stocks as "POJ"—Piece Of Junk—and "POS "—figure it out yourself), the chief executive of Merrill Lynch, David Komansky, issued a belated apology. But the bottom line remained: Merrill, as investment banker, earned large commissions from the sale of shares to gullible investors who bought their advice in addition to the huge sums they made from the undeservingly hyped companies by way of investment banking fees.

Analysts aren't necessarily bad, but they may become blinded. Read what they have to say, supplement that with your own research, and don't put full trust in those who can be influenced by their own interests.

"I am not a man of words." (Exodus 4:10)

Can you guess who made this self-deprecating remark, alluding to his speech impediment? Holy Moses, you're right! It was none other than the man selected by God to be the first rabbi in history! Moses was the man entrusted with leadership, and yet he lacked not only eloquence but even the most basic ability to clearly enunciate words. As he himself put it, in attempting to decline the mission God imposed upon him, "for I am slow of speech, and slow of tongue."

According to some commentators, Moses' problem was that he stuttered. Others claim that his handicap was a serious lisp. In any event, it seems very strange that God would select someone so obviously lacking a fundamental quality of leadership. And if Moses' other qualities compensated for this failing, ask the commentators, why didn't God simply cure him? Why did God choose a man "not of words" to become "the Great Communicator" of His will?

The answer most frequently given is that *God didn't want a man of words; He preferred a man of action.* Those gifted with speech often use it as a substitute for deeds. It was the greatest leader of the Jewish people whose role was to demonstrate the truth of the adage that, "Actions speak louder than words."

As the anonymous nursery rhyme puts it:

A man of words and not of deeds
Is like a garden full of weeds.

What we are to learn from this story is to judge people not by what they say but by what they do. How relevant this idea is to us today was made clear by a feature story on the front page of the business section of the Sunday *New York Times* of May 27, 2001. The headline said it all: "Buy, They Say. But What Do They Do?"

Gretchen Morgenson, the author of the article, tells the story of a senior e-commerce analyst who published a list of nine stocks that he said held the greatest promise for investors in the coming year. That was on September 11 of 2000, and one of the stocks on the list was iBasis, a provider of Internet telephony services whose initial public offering, and secondary one, had both been managed by his firm, Robertson Stephens. The stock, which sold for $21 that September day, had traded as high as $49 in June.

"We believe that the recent pullback in the market has created an attractive entry point for investors to expand or establish a position in what we believe will be dominant market leaders," the analyst wrote, reiterating his buy recommendation on iBasis.

Just over two months later, on November 27, with the stock at $5.25, the analyst *filed to sell thousands of his own shares*.

Even as he sold the shares—and two other executives at Robbie Stephens did the same—the analyst did not waver in his public support for the stock. Ms. Morgenson goes on to cite numerous instances in which other firms dumped shares of a stock they were simultaneously recommending to their clients. Their words said one thing, their actions another.

"The superior man," Confucius wrote, "speaks according to his actions." But on Wall Street, talking the talk doesn't always equate to walking the walk. Alice in Wonderland wasn't sure "whether you *can* make words mean so many different things." Unfortunately, we live in a time when they do—at least for some people. "Buy" recommendations may be appropriate, but it's better to look at what a person *does* than what he *tells you* to do.

Cast your bread upon the waters, for you shall find it after many days (Ecclesiastes 11:1).

Here's the last bit of advice from the Bible I'm going to give you. It's not so much a warning as it is an insurance policy. In almost all faiths, man is a steward for God. We are meant to be charitable so that we assist in the Divine Plan of distributing money to the needy.

When you make money in the market, be sure to take some of your profits and give it to a worthy cause. That way, God sees that you are a good manager of His wealth and the Bible promises that He will, for that reason, bless you with more.

The religious term for this concept is tithing. It requires that we set aside 10 percent of our gains to do good works with them.

Ask yourself honestly if, when you had your fortune, you followed this rule. Actually it's not giving anything away, because it comes with a promise from God that He will return it multifold.

The words of Ecclesiastes prove themselves true not only in financial matters. They are a magnificent guide to the way in which we should lead our lives. When we do for others, and cast our bread upon the waters, we *will* find it returned after many days. Let me conclude this chapter with an inspirational story that illustrates it best:

Many years ago, a wealthy family in England took their children for a holiday into the country. Their host turned over his estate to the visitors for the weekend. The children went swimming in a pool. As one of the boys began to drown, the other boys screamed for help. The son of the gardener jumped into the pool and rescued the lad who was going under.

Later, the grateful parents asked the gardener what they could do for the young hero. The gardener said his son wanted to go to college some day. "He wants to be a doctor," said the gardener. The visitors shook hands on that. "We'll be glad to pay his way through," they said.

Years later, Winston Churchill was stricken with pneumonia. The King of England instructed that the best doctor be found to save the Prime Minister. That doctor turned out to be Alexander Fleming, the developer of penicillin. Churchill recovered soon after.

"Rarely," said Churchill later, "has one man owed his life twice to the same rescuer." Sir Alexander was the gardener's son and Churchill was the boy who nearly drowned in that pool long before.

The good that we do, be it through money or acts of kindness, will eventually be repaid to us in one form or another. And that, I assure you, is a promise from the Bible.

— What You Want to Remember —

■ The Bible is more than a religious work. Its insights and teachings can guide us financially, helping us not to repeat previous mistakes and to invest successfully.

■ Wise people should take to heart the discovery of Joseph in his interpretation of Pharaoh's dream: The economy is governed by cycles of boom and bust. All those who have ever maintained that, "This time it's different," disregard the biblical assurance that "There is nothing new under the sun."

- Borrowing, according to the Bible, turns you into a slave of the lender. Buying on margin is nothing more than enslaving yourself for the future.

- Not only individuals but nations as well are warned by God not to be excessive borrowers. Even the most powerful countries and the strongest economies can fall victim to the perils of irrational debt.

- The herd mentality can cause tulips to cost more than a house and Internet companies on the verge of bankruptcy to sell at astronomical prices.

- Self-interest, like a bribe, prevents people from making fair and honest judgments. Be wary of those recommending stocks who must tell you to buy in order to continue to make a living.

- Listen far more to what people themselves do than what they say.

- Always take some of your profits and use them for charitable works. The Bible promises that is the source of all blessing, and whatever you give away you will get back many times over.

- Review all the biblical quotes in this chapter. Then reflect on the words of Henry Lord Beecher: ''The Bible is God's chart for you to steer by, to keep you from the bottom of the sea, and to show you where the harbor is, and how to reach it without running on rocks or bars.''

Notes

1. James Dale Davidson and Sir William Rees-Mogg, *Blood in the Streets* (New York: Simon & Schuster, 1987).
2. Warren Buffett, as quoted in *Fortune* Magazine, November 22, 1999.

3. Davidson and Rees-Mogg, *Blood in the Streets.*

4. Harold Evans, *The American Century* (New York: Alfred Knopf, 1998).

5. Gregory Zuckerman, "Borrowing Levels Reach a Record, Sparking Debate," *Wall Street Journal*, July 5, 2000, p. C1.

CHAPTER 20

Starting Over

*The past is but the
beginning of a beginning.*

—H. G. Wells

Psychologists and clergymen agree: Grief isn't meant to last forever. "Grief," as the British prime minister Benjamin Disraeli noted, "is the agony of an instant; the indulgence of grief, the blunder of a life."

In Jewish tradition, there is a remarkable ritual observed in the aftermath of the death of a loved one. First, the members of the family "sit *shiva*" for seven days (the meaning of the word *shiva*), they remain at home and mourn their parent, spouse, sibling, or child as friends come to visit and offer comfort and consolation. For everything there is a season, and seven days are reserved for weeping and reflecting on all that was and is no more. When the *shiva* comes to a close, however, the mourners are obligated to step out of the house and walk around the block. Symbolically, they give expression to the idea that life must go on. Loss makes us despair. Hope brings us healing.

Professor Benjamin Barber, a political scientist at Rutgers University and an astute social observer, advises everyone forced to deal with life's tragedies to "sit *shiva*," to set aside an appropriate time for mourning and then walk out into the sunshine and make plans to begin life anew.

The goal is not to forget the past. It is to move on in spite of it. The past is history. It is meant to be remembered. The future is destiny. It is meant to be dealt with creatively and optimistically. As Charles Kettering put it so well: "My interest is in the future because I am going to spend the rest of my life there."

Stopping a Suicide

It was one of the most difficult moments of my life. I was teaching a class when a dormitory counselor burst in and told me he desperately needed my help. One of my students was in his room threatening to kill himself. None of his friends could talk him out of it. Perhaps, they thought, that I, as his rabbi, might be able to reach him.

I rushed to his room. He was even more despondent than I could have imagined. Crying bitterly, he told me that his girlfriend had just broken up with him. She was absolutely perfect, he explained. He had been sure they were soul mates, and they would, in the not-too-distant future, get married and raise a family. What point was there in going on without her? How could he find any purpose for his existence without the love of his life?

I spent hours trying to convince him that he could find happiness again. It took the rest of the day and all of the next night for me to finally calm him down to the point where I was sure that he would no longer do anything drastic.

Twenty years passed. Once again, in the middle of my teaching a class, there was a knock on the door. When I opened it, a handsome, middle-aged man stood before me and asked, "Do you remember me, Rabbi?" With a sudden flash of recognition, I immediately answered, "Yes, of course—and you owe me a night's sleep."

The former student who so long ago tried to commit suicide had come back to tell me the end of the story. Shortly after his break-up, he met another girl, so wonderful, so kind, so overflowing with character and personality, that he wondered what he possibly could have seen in his "first great love." "Today," he continued, "I am married to this truly perfect woman I would never even have met were it not for what I considered my tragic break-up. We have three beautiful children and what I can only describe as an ideal family life. To top it off, I just recently learned that my first flame has been married and divorced three times, leaving behind her a trail of adulterous affairs. Today I see that break-up as the greatest blessing of my life."

Then he concluded with these words: "I've come back to thank you for teaching me the most important lesson of life: That we can always start over, no matter how bad a situation seems at the time."

Nobody Said It's Easy

"Come on, cheer up, it's not really so bad." "Don't take it so hard." No matter how well intentioned, these clichés are bad advice, and implicit criticism. Psychologists warn us that the worst way to try to help someone cope with a tragedy is to diminish its importance. That only makes your friends feel worse—as if they don't even deserve your sympathy.

"That's easy for you to say," the person suffering might snap back, and they would be right. As Mel Brooks put it so well, "Minor surgery is your operation; major surgery is mine." Applied to the economy, the same thought has been put this way: A recession is when your neighbor loses his job; a depression is when you get fired.

That's why I don't want you to think that I'm minimizing your pain. You *can* start over in life—but nobody can promise you that it's going to be easy.

Still, there is comfort in knowing that the widow can someday find another partner who will make her happy. Survivors of bitter divorces *can* start over and meet partners more suitable for them. Even parents who have lost a child can move on with their lives—because they have no alternative, because to remain in perpetual depression is to ruin their lives and the lives of their other children as well, and because you never know what the future holds in store for you.

When Shakespeare's Macbeth asks the doctor whether he can prescribe "some sweet oblivious antidote" to a sorrowing heart, the doctor answers: "Therein the patient must minister to himself."

No, nobody says it's easy. But history shows that it's possible even after the most horrible catastrophes. To prove it to ourselves, all we have to do is reflect upon the seminal event of the twentieth century.

Survivors

In a previous market downturn, Alan "Ace" Greenberg, chairman of Bear Stearns, wrote the following to his staff in his *Memos from the Chairman*: "Some people for ethnic reasons get through this period easier than others. For example, I have never felt better or slept sounder, but I do have an advantage over some of my peers at other firms—I am the beneficiary of five thousand years of persecution. This market will not get me down. It is just a minor challenge."

As a Jew, Greenberg felt he could more readily put the fluctuations of the stock market in perspective. Jewish history had taught him that life often requires us to start all over again.

What was valid in the past is even more painfully true today. Six million Jews were tortured in the most sadistic and unimaginable ways, beaten to death, burned alive, and literally worked to death.

Amazingly enough, in spite of Hitler's plan for a "Final Solution" ridding the world of all Jews, there were some who survived. Left without homes, for the most part without families and without any money, they found places of haven around the world. They truly started over from nothing. And a significant percentage of them succeeded beyond anyone's wildest dreams. They started new families. They amassed considerable wealth. They became communal leaders.

As a friend of mine, Shoshana Comet, a professional counselor who works with Holocaust survivors, said to me: "Holocaust survivors should never be referred to as victims. Indeed they are victors." They overcame the unimaginable and then they achieved the impossible.

What is the secret of their success? What can we learn from the ways in which they were able to start over? What was the source of their strength? What inspiration can we derive from their heroic stories?

The person I believe who best answered these crucial questions is Viktor Frankl. An eminent psychiatrist, Frankl was imprisoned at Auschwitz and other concentration camps for three years during the Second World War. Surrounded by suffering and loss, Frankl began to wonder why some of his fellow prisoners were better able to cope than others. His conclusion became the basis of his book, *Man's Search for Meaning*, originally published in 1959, which Carl Rogers called "one of the outstanding contributions to psychological thought in the last fifty years." Since publication, it has become a classic that sold more than four million copies in English language editions alone. The Library of Congress hails it as "one of the ten most influential books in America."[1]

What was Frankl's daring and original conclusion? Unlike Freud, who believed that sexual instincts and urges are the driving force of humanity, Frankl pioneered the idea that man's deepest desire is to search for meaning and purpose. "The will to meaning" became the basis of his groundbreaking psychological theory, logotherapy. Its major maxim, as Nietzsche put it, is "He who has a why to live for can bear almost any how."

"Our generation is realistic, for we have come to know man as he really is," Frankl writes. "After all, man is that being who invented the gas chambers of Auschwitz; however, he is also that being who entered those gas chambers upright with the Lord's Prayer or the *Shema Yisrael* (Hear O Israel, the Lord is our God, the Lord is one) on his lips."

Frankl makes clear that the ones who survived understood

that "the most difficult parts of life are dealt with best not by giving in, but by clinging to meaning behind any struggle." In one of the many beautiful passages in the book, Frankl states, "What is demanded of man is not, as some existential philosophers teach, to endure the meaninglessness of life; but rather to bear his incapacity to grasp its unconditional meaningfulness in rational terms."

Perhaps most relevant to all of us is Frankl's assertion, after living through the horrors of hell, that "Everything can be taken from a man but one thing: the last of the human freedoms—to choose one's attitude in any given set of circumstances, to choose one's own way."

Frankl gives new meaning to the phrase "starting over" with his suggestions guided by the approach of logotherapy:

- You cannot avoid suffering, but you can change your attitude toward it, to give suffering a meaning to you.

- Live your life as though you were living it the second time. New life has a series of movie frames, whose ending and meaning aren't apparent until the very conclusion of the film; yet, each of the hundreds of individual frames has meaning within the context of the whole film.

- View your life backwards, as if from your funeral. Review your life experiences. Ask yourself what you have accomplished. What would you have wanted to accomplish but didn't? What were your happiest moments? What were the saddest? What would you do again and what wouldn't you?

- Now that you still have more of your life before you, how will you give it meaning?

What logotherapy makes clear is that people do not die all at once. Instead, they pass away in stages. As life continues to lose meaning for them, they almost visibly fade before our eyes. Survivors share the secret of maintaining their dignity and self-esteem no matter what their external conditions. Survivors are gifted with faith, hope, and an optimistic spirit. Survivors hold on to their sense of humor, because they realize that if they cannot laugh they will only weep, and find no reason to go on living. Survivors believe that they are here on earth for some purpose and that their lives have meaning. That is why they want so very much to survive—and that's what had made it possible for so many of them to *thrive*.

Even God Started Over

Kabbalah is the study of Jewish mysticism. In it are discussions of secrets not revealed in the Bible but transmitted orally throughout the ages by holy scholars. One of its teachings reveals a remarkable tradition about the creation of the world.

This earth, say the masters of the *Kabbalah*, is not the first one to have been brought into being by God. The opening word of the Bible, in fact, alludes to this fact. In Hebrew, the Five Books of Moses begin with the word *B'rayshit*—"In the beginning." The first letter of the opening word, the *Bet*—in English, "B,"—is the *second* letter of the Hebrew alphabet, as it is in the English alphabet.

The mystics ask why the Bible doesn't begin its description of Creation with the very first letter of the alphabet, the *aleph*, or "A." They answer that this is God's way of hinting that ours is not the first world He created.

God made worlds, destroyed them, and then *started all over again*.

Everything God did, the mystics continue, is to teach us by example how to live our lives. Whatever He did is meant to inspire us to act in similar manner. At the very beginning of the Bible, then, God is guiding us to follow in His ways: When the world around us crumbles, we also must find the courage to create anew.

To all those who say, "My world is over," God replies, "Then do as I did and rebuild another."

Persevere–and Perfect

Starting over in many situations provides you with advantages you didn't have the first time. If your world that was destroyed involved your business, your job, your investments, or your stock portfolio, surely you are smarter now than you were the last time around. You must have learned something from your terrible experience. Starting again doesn't mean simply doing it over—but doing it better.

An unknown author summarized the story of life in these five very short chapters:

Chapter 1. I walk down a street and there's a deep hole in the sidewalk. I fall in. It takes forever to get out. It's not my fault.

Chapter 2. I walk down the same street. I fall in the hole again. It still takes a long time to get out. It's not completely my fault. I forgot.

Chapter 3. I walk down the same street. I fall in the hole again. It's becoming a habit. It is my fault. I get out immediately.

Chapter 4. I walk down the same street and see the deep hole in the sidewalk. I walk around it.

Chapter 5. I walk down a different street.

At some point all of us do learn from experience. As Welsh composer Grace Williams observed: "A man never wakes up his second baby just to see it smile." Only a cynic will tell you that the sole benefit of experience is that it enables you to recognize a mistake when you make it again. The truth is that wisdom is the scar tissue of experience. That's why once you've suffered the pain, you're prepared to savor the gain.

Learn from the Stars

If only we all could be like the tennis great Billie Jean King. As her former tennis partner and now sports psychologist, Julie Anthony, recounts, "Billie Jean once told me that whenever she misses a shot, she never starts the next point until she has mentally corrected what she did wrong on that shot. She goes over the bad stroke in her mind and analyzes what she did wrong and then actually takes the correct swing in the air so that she wipes out the negative imprint and replaces it with a positive one."[2]

Successful athletes call it "instant reinterpretation." They know that if you hit nine wonderful shots in tennis, for example, and you miss the last one, you don't remember the nine good shots, but only the one that you missed. The more you mentally rehearse the shot that failed, the more you're imprinting it on your mind. That way you're giving more weight to the negative than to the positive. The way to overcome that, in sports as well as in life, is to immediately reinterpret and rethink events in a positive way.

Julie Anthony tells of the time she was with Billie Jean when she played at the finals at Wimbledon. For twelve months Billie Jean had been preparing for this tournament. Finally she went out and played—and lost miserably.

Julie describes what she saw next: "I was sitting in the locker room, and I thought she would probably come back and announce she was going into retirement again or planning to commit suicide. Instead she came in and totally surprised me with her attitude. She was hitting the walls and the lockers and slapping her hands and saying, 'God, I can't wait till next year, I'm going to do it next year. I know what I did wrong.' She was already correcting her mistakes, psyching herself up to keep playing. I thought the loss was going to be a failure to her. To her, the loss was simply a loss. That's probably why she was a champion and I wasn't. She could take a loss and not let it get her down. She could rebound quicker and get on with the positive. When she came into the locker room, she was already thinking about what she had to work on specifically to improve the deficits in her game so she could win the next one."[3]

It's not only athletes who know this secret. When the noted Danish sculptor, Bertel Thorwaldsen, was once asked by an admirer, "Which do you consider your greatest statue?" he responded without hesitation, "My next one."

Who Says It's Impossible?

Chaim Weizmann, the first president of the State of Israel, was fond of repeating this aphorism: "Difficulties take a long time to solve. The impossible always takes a little longer."

Look carefully at the word "impossible" and you'll notice that of its ten letters, eighty percent make the word "possible." If you were successful once, you can be successful again. All it takes is for *you* to believe it. For example, Henry Flagler made a modest fortune in his youth and then went bankrupt in the salt business before making a vast fortune with Standard Oil. As Elihu Root put it, "Men do not fail; they give up trying."

When John Jacob Astor learned that his largest investment, a fur-trading post called (what else?) Astoria in the Oregon wilderness, had been wiped out by the fortunes of war, he went to the theater that night anyway. When a friend expressed surprise at seeing him there, Astor merely answered, "What would you have me do? Would you have me stay at home and weep for what I cannot help?" And when the show was over, Astor immediately started all over again. He ignored the misfortune he couldn't help—and created a second and even larger fortune the next time around.

It isn't true that lightning doesn't strike twice. Some of the greatest success stories began after people lost everything they had. And that can be the reality for you as well. Your life is far from over if you only remember the wisdom of the popular saying that "Today is the first day of the rest of your life."

When the Sunday school teacher asked his young pupil,

"Michael, who made you?," the immediate answer was: "I don't really know. I ain't done yet."

Whenever we're down or depressed, that's what we have to remember. "We ain't done yet"—and the rest of our story can be more blessed than it ever was before.

⟶ What You Want to Remember ⟵

- Mourning isn't meant to last forever. We need to walk around the block and resume our lives after "sitting *shiva*."

- Tragedies deeply wound, but time heals—if we only let it.

- People survived and started their lives over again even after the Holocaust. Beginning with absolutely nothing, many of them became highly successful and highlight the power of human potential.

- Viktor Frankl pioneered the approach of logotherapy to explain the unique attributes of those who were able to overcome the horrors of their surroundings and even prosper. His major conclusion was that man's search for meaning in life is what allows for hope, faith, humor, and the will to live.

- The *Kabbalah* teaches us that this is not the first world. God created, destroyed, and then created again. Now that God has shown us that it's possible, we too have to rebuild whenever it seems our personal lives have been destroyed.

- Athletes, artists, and masters in every field know the importance of learning from temporary setbacks and look forward to starting over and doing better in the future. Experience is the teacher that ensures we can not only start over again but also do it better the next time.

■ It's true that God made us, but after that we have to share the responsibility with Him and continue to make ourselves as well.

Notes

1. Victor Frankel, *Man's Search for Meaning* (Boston: Beacon Press, 2000).
2. Julie Anthony, as quoted in Carole Hyatt and Linda Gottlieb, *When Smart People Fail* (New York: Simon & Schuster, 1987), p. 134.
3. Ibid.

CHAPTER 21

The Fortune You're Going to Leave Behind

*The purpose of life is
not to be happy, but to matter.*

—Leo Rosten,
twentieth-century American
author and scholar

We all want to leave a legacy. Much of the reason for our strong desire to accumulate wealth—and our sorrow at losing it—comes from our deep-seated need to be remembered once we depart this world.

Now here's an interesting question for you to consider: What would you rather leave to your children—Kodak stock or Kodak moments? Money or memories? I don't think there's any question. Money lasts for a little while and is spent. Memories live on forever and serve as everlasting reminders of our existence. Money is reduced by inflation; memories are intensified by time. Money is called currency, but only memories remain current.

The Israeli poet Yehuda Amichai said it beautifully in his poem, "Candles That Remember":

There are candles that remember for twenty-four hours,
As the label says. And there are candles
that remember for eight hours.
And there are eternal candles that promise
the memory of a man to his sons.

When You Weren't Looking

Memories are created every moment. Some of the most important ones are even made when you're totally unaware. And
these, very often, are really the most valuable legacies you can
leave to your children. This is the real fortune you'll be hand-
ing over to future generations, worth even more than Bill
Gates' portfolio.

These words were written by a child whose identity is unfortunately unknown. Its insights, however, speak profoundly
to every parent:

When you thought I wasn't looking, I saw you hang my first
painting on the refrigerator, and I immediately wanted to
paint another one.
When you thought I wasn't looking, I saw you feed a stray
cat, and I learned that it was good to be kind to animals.
When you thought I wasn't looking, I saw you make my
favorite cake for me and I learned that the little things can be
the special things in life.
When you thought I wasn't looking, I heard you say a prayer,
and I knew there is a God I could always talk to and I learned
to trust in God.
When you thought I wasn't looking, I saw you make a meal
and take it to a friend who was sick, and I learned that we
all have to help take care of each other.
When you thought I wasn't looking, I saw you give of your
time and money to help people who had nothing and I

learned that those who have something should give to those who don't.

When you thought I wasn't looking, I felt you kiss me goodnight and I felt loved and safe.

When you thought I wasn't looking, I saw you take care of our house and everyone in it and I learned we have to take care of what we are given.

When you thought I wasn't looking, I saw how you handled your responsibilities, even when you didn't feel good, and I learned that I would have to be responsible when I grow up.

When you thought I wasn't looking, I saw tears come from your eyes and I learned that sometimes things hurt, but it's all right to cry.

When you thought I wasn't looking, I saw that you cared and I wanted to be everything that I could be.

When you thought I wasn't looking, I learned most of life's lessons that I need to know to be a good and productive person when I grow up.

When you thought I wasn't looking, I looked at you and wanted to say, "Thanks for all the things I saw when you thought I wasn't looking."

Memories Born of Discovery

Sometimes parents don't know how to communicate their love. Their silence is mistaken for callousness and a cold relationship follows. All the money in the world cannot undo the bitterness of misunderstanding. But what dollars cannot do, memories can sometimes accomplish even after death.

Let me share with you a deeply moving experience I had some time ago.

I officiated at the memorial service of a father of one of my congregants. At the funeral home, the congregant informed me that he would not be saying *Kaddish* (the traditional prayer that mourners are obligated to recite for the dead) for his father and asked if I could make arrangements to have someone paid to do it for him. I complied with his wishes, but found myself surprised a week or two later to see him walk into the chapel for services, at which time he rose to recite the *Kaddish*. I didn't want to say anything. I didn't want to make him feel uncomfortable for doing the right thing. But after seeing him return two or three more times, my curiosity got the best of me. I just had to know what was going on. And so I approached him and told him how good it was to see him and how fortunate it was that he had discovered that he could find the time and arrange his schedule to be in the synagogue for the *Kaddish*.

His response took me by surprise: "Rabbi, the time and my schedule were never the issues. I didn't want to say *Kaddish* for my father. Forgive me for saying it, but I really didn't think he deserved it. I never felt that I had much of a relationship with him. I felt that all my life I had tried in every which way to win his attention, his affection, his approval, and I never got it. He always seemed so distant, so caught up in himself and his work. I still remember when I was in the fifth grade we had a contest to see who could make the best paper plane. Mine came in first. I was so excited and proud. I drew the word 'Dad' on its side and brought it home and presented it to him. All he did was just about acknowledge it. And that was it! And for me that always symbolized our relationship. My doing all that I could to win his approval and affection, him just about acknowledging it; and that was it. And so when he passed away, excuse me for sounding so immature, but I just couldn't get myself to say the *Kaddish*. Why should I, I thought."

And then came the tears. "Rabbi, a few days after his funeral we went down to his office to clean out his desk. I opened the top drawer and there was the paper airplane. As I took it in my hand and stared at it, his secretary commented on how many times my father had done the exact same thing. Always with a proud smile on his face."

Parents may not always be perfect. But rather than focus on those imperfections, if we could just reflect on their sacrifices, their gifts, their love, their concern, and their devotion, we would finally realize that we were left a Last Will and Testament worth far more than a portfolio of blue chip stocks.

Memories, Doughnuts, and Michael Jackson

That message is something that one of the contemporary super-stars of the entertainment industry confesses he recently learnt. What could the father of a billionaire possibly leave of value to his son? Michael Jackson poignantly reveals what really matters to a child. He writes:

> When I look back on my childhood, it is not an idyllic landscape of memories. My relationship with my father was strained, and my childhood was an emotionally difficult time for me. I began performing when I was five years old, and my father—a tough man—pushed my brothers and me hard, from the earliest age, to be the best performers we could be.
>
> Although we all worked hard to perform, he never really complimented me. If I did a great show, he would tell me it was a good show. And if I did an OK show, he didn't say anything at all. He seemed intent, above all else, on making us a commercial success.
>
> My father was not openly affectionate with us, but he would show his love in different ways. I remember once when I was about four years old, we were at a little carnival and he picked me up and put me on a pony. It was a tiny gesture, probably something he forgot five minutes later. But because of that one moment, I have this special place in my heart for him. Because that's how kids are, the little things mean so much to them and for me, that one moment meant everything. It was a gesture that showed his caring,

and his love. I only experienced it that one time, but it made me feel really good, about him and the world.

And I have other memories too, of other gestures, however imperfect, that showed his love for us. When I was a kid, I had a real sweet tooth—we all did. I loved eating glazed doughnuts, and my father knew that. So every few weeks I would come downstairs in the morning and there on the kitchen counter was a bag of glazed doughnuts—no note of explanation, just the doughnuts. It was like a fairy godmother had visited our kitchen. It was like Santa Claus. Sometimes, I would think about staying up late so I could see him leave them there, but as with Santa Claus, I didn't want to ruin the magic, for fear that he would never do it again.

I think now that my father had to leave the doughnuts secretly at night so that no one would catch him with his guard down. He was scared of human emotion, he didn't understand it, or know how to deal with it. But, he did know doughnuts.

With hindsight and maturity, I have come to see that even my father's harshness was a kind of love. An imperfect love, sure, but love nonetheless. He pushed me because he loved me. He pushed me because he wanted me to have more than he EVER had, and he wanted my life to be better than his EVER was.

It has taken me a long time to realize this, but now I feel the resentments of my childhood are finally being put to rest. My bitterness has been replaced by blessing, and in place of my anger, I have found absolution. And with this knowledge, that my father loved his children, I have found peace.[1]

So here's a suggestion if you lost almost all of your money in the market: Buy your kids some doughnuts—and they'll probably remember you at least as much as if you had left them "dough"!

For Those Who Don't Understand

It seems so obvious. Memories are worth more than money. Tragically enough, though, our obsession with wealth sometimes blinds us to what is really valuable.

Not long ago, I was browsing in an antique store when I spotted an all-too-familiar object. How could I not know immediately what it was when I had been so involved in its story? After all, my eulogy of Sam, a survivor of the infamous Auschwitz concentration camp, focused on it.

What a tale it had been. The Germans had rounded up all the Jews in his little town for deportation. Others may have believed the grand lie that they were merely being transported to another site to be used for labor. Sam was too smart for that. He knew that they were meant to be murdered. He understood that the Nazis wanted to eliminate every Jew as well as every reminder of their religious heritage. So Sam took a chance. Had he been caught, he would have paid with his life. But he did what he had to do so that something might remain—so that even if not a single Jew in the world stayed alive someone might find it, reflect, and remember.

He wished he could have hidden much more. How he wanted to preserve a scroll of the Bible or a holy synagogue vessel. But he had so little time, so little space for concealing an object of value. His choice, in retrospect, seemed almost divinely inspired for its symbolism. It was a silver Passover plate used to commemorate the ancient festival of freedom. Perhaps, Sam thought with what he later conceded was far too much optimism, miracles could once more occur even in modern times. And from that day forward not a day went by in the hells of the concentration camps that his mind did not return to his Seder plate in its special hiding place.

Sam could never explain how he of all his family and friends survived. In his heart of hearts, he once confided to me, it may have been because he viewed his continued existence on earth as a holy mission—to go back to his roots and uncover his own symbol of survival. Incredibly enough, the escapee of twentieth-century genocide was reunited with his ritual reminder of deliverance from age-old Egyptian oppression. Sam retrieved his Seder plate and celebrated dozens of Passovers with it until his recent death.

That, in almost total disbelief, is what I saw in the shop for sale. Where was it from, I inquired? How did the owner come to have it? Oh, I was told, it was part of the sale of the contents of an estate by the children. You see, the deceased was religious but his descendants aren't—so they don't really have any need for "items like these."

Indeed, this wasn't the first time I discovered that we live in an age that doesn't understand the meaning of memories or the concept of keepsakes. How I wish that the unsentimental harshness of Sam's descendants was just an aberration, a remarkably unusual demonstration of insensitivity not likely to be duplicated by others. But the sad truth is that we are part of a "throwaway" culture that gives equal weight to used cars, worn furniture, and old family treasures. What has served the past is of no interest if its sole claim to respectability is its gift of associations.

"Unless we remember," English novelist Edward Morgan Foster put it so beautifully, "we cannot understand." The past leaves its message robed in the simplest of garments. They are the soul of those very things with which we come into daily contact. And they possess the unique ability of stirring up memories that keep alive those whom we deeply loved. Dishes on which we shared festive meals. Pictures we looked at together and understood in a way no one else did. The silver cup my father gave me when he told me I was "now a man" and he expected great things of me. The trinkets we purchased that summer we always call the best vacation of our lives. The first toy of our first child. How can such inexpensive objects bring me so much pleasure—or sadness? It is foolish to think of what we have as possessions. We do not own them as much as they have a claim upon us.

Every so often the newspapers carry a story of a rummage

sale that brings a surprised buyer unexpected riches. Unwittingly someone sells a valuable painting for a pittance, an irreplaceable antique, a one-of-a-kind object. The frustrated owner bemoans the fact that he was unaware of the object's true value. But what makes him unhappy is only the knowledge that he could have gotten more for it. It is the world's valuation that shocks him. Yet he still fails to realize that so much more of what he gave away for pennies had priceless worth for him if he would have but taken the time to see it. "The heart hath its own memory, like the mind," Longfellow taught us, "and in it are enshrined the precious keepsakes."

Memorabilia have lost their allure because we no longer revere the meaning of memories. So what, I am often asked, if my grandparents used this every holiday? We have no space, we have no need for it. As if utilitarian function is the only rationale for holding on to something that enables us to preserve our past!

The ring with which I married my wife may not be the most expensive but I pray it remains in my family as a legacy of the love we shared, perhaps to be used again by my grandchildren. The cup with which I usher in the sanctity of every Sabbath may reflect the poverty of my youth, but I hope it is passed on to the future as a testament to the importance of religious values in our household. If what we treasured is held sacred by my children, then perhaps what we lived for will also be reverentially recalled.

That's why I will weep for my friend Sam as well as for all those whose families don't understand this simple truth: To discard our physical links with the past is to be guilty of a most insidious form of murder—the murder of memory.

Some Final Advice

In closing, let me leave you, my fellow victims of financial distress, with the following advice.

Save your children's airplanes, and pray that they save your Seder plates. Put them on ponies, and they will put you on pedestals. Appreciate what's truly valuable and then, just when you have taught your children as well as yourself that money doesn't matter, God will say, "When you thought I wasn't looking, I was—and now you deserve to prosper once more."

⏜ What You Want to Remember ⏜

- If you must choose between leaving your children money or memories, always pick memories. That will leave them with a fortune far more meaningful than money.

- Memories are created every moment by all the things that we, as parents, do—and which our children carefully observe.

- Sometimes parents have difficulty verbalizing their love. Their legacy should include remembrance of their special acts of kindness and their pride in our achievements, even if we learn of them after their deaths.

- Some people today don't comprehend the value of mementos and keepsakes. For them, cash is king and memories of little concern. They are destined to discover the folly of their error.

- Don't give up on your dream of becoming rich once more. But don't feel as if you've failed if you can pass on meaningful memories to your future generations.

Note

1. Michael Jackson, "Memories of My Childhood," *Olam,* Summer 2001, p. 9.

Are You Feeling Better Now?

Prescriptions for Each Day of the Week

All the good maxims have been written.
It only remains to put them into practice.

—Blaise Pascal

There's an old Hindu proverb that says, "The patient does not recover health by hearing the medicine described." What you've read until now represents the combined wisdom of some of the greatest minds in all of history. The advice I've shared with you comes from the most ancient of religions, as well as the most contemporary findings of modern psychology.

None of it will help, however, if the accumulated knowledge of the ages isn't invited to enter your heart and your soul. A doctor's prescription can save your life—but only if you fill it and scrupulously follow its directions.

The problem, as the dean emeritus of Harvard Law School, Roscoe Pound, reminds us, is that "When you read, *read*! Too many students just half read. I never read without summarizing—and so understanding what I read. The art of memory is the art of understanding."

To read this book correctly requires courage. The courage to admit mistakes. The courage to be willing to listen to the advice of those who have become masters of their fate, rather than its victims. The courage to have the will to keep standing up even after being counted out. The courage to demonstrate, in the profound words of Ernest Hemingway, "grace under pressure."

For every one of you, a different chapter will have more meaning and relevance. "I know," said a great sage to the reader of one of his books, "which one of the chapters you liked the most." "But I didn't tell you," his disciple said with amazement. "I didn't mean," replied the sage, "that I can identify the chapter by number. I only mean that I am certain the chapter you most appreciated is the one whose ideas you *needed* the most."

The truths we most require to take to heart are thankfully the ones that find the straightest and fastest route to our souls.

I urge you now to reread the book one more time with pen or pencil in hand. Mark the portions that speak to *you!* Try to memorize the ideas that resonate with greatest intensity and clarity. Before you go to bed every night, don't only count your blessings and pray. Mentally review the new priorities and perspectives you've gained and consider how they relate to your life.

Take One a Day for a Full Week

I'm going to leave you with seven messages. Every one of them can change your life—if you let it. Set aside some moments every day. Read that day's lesson. Don't try to read them all at once because you won't have time to reflect and fully absorb the message. Just like medicine, an overdose might prove to be counterproductive.

To make sure that you remember every day's insight, I highly recommend that you repeat it to at least two friends.

When you're done with your homework for the week, I promise that you will no longer feel weak or depressed. You'll find the spiritual therapy you need to make yourself a happier, more productive, and more successful person. You will realize that the best maxim of life is to live to one's maximum. In the words of inspirational author Ben Sweetland, "Success is a journey, not a destination." Live by the teachings of those who have discovered how best to weather the stormy seas, and I guarantee you a lifelong cruise filled with joy until you reach your heavenly port.

The Message for Sunday

It wasn't yours in the first place.

The second-century scholar, Rabbi Meir, was giving a lecture at the synagogue one Sabbath afternoon. At the very same time, unbeknown to him, his two beloved sons suddenly died. The grief-stricken mother, Beruriah, covered them with a sheet and waited until her husband came home after the Sabbath.

When Rabbi Meir arrived and asked where his sons were, his wife begged her husband to first recite the *Havdalah* service marking the departure of the Sabbath. Then, she said, she had a very important question to ask him. Perplexed, but nonetheless acceding to his wife's wishes, Rabbi Meir recited the prayer and then asked his wife to tell him her problem. She said: " Not long ago, some precious jewels were entrusted to my care. Now the owner of the jewels has come to reclaim them. Shall I return them to him?"

Rabbi Meir was surprised by the simplicity of the question and his wife's need to ask him for guidance. "But of course," he said, "you yourself know the law very well. An object entrusted for a time must be given back when the owner demands it."

Beruriah then took her husband by the hand, led him to where the dead children lay and drew back the sheet. Rabbi Meir began to weep uncontrollably. "My sons! My sons!" he cried.

Then Beruriah reminded him tearfully of his own words: "Didn't you say that we must restore to the owner what he entrusted to our care? Our sons were the jewels that God allowed us to have for some years. Now their Master has taken back His own gifts to us. Let us, even at this tragic moment of loss, feel gratitude for the gift God gave us in all the time we were blessed to have these jewels, our precious children."

The moral: Always remember that whatever you have is a gift from God. If it's taken from you, don't curse the loss; thank God for however much time you were given to be blessed by His gifts.

Message for Monday

Milk can be worth more than money.

One day, a poor boy who was selling goods from door to door to pay his way through school found he had only one thin dime left, and he was hungry. He decided he would ask for a meal at the next house. However, he lost his nerve when a lovely young woman opened the door. Instead of a meal he asked for a drink of water.

She thought he looked hungry so she brought him a large glass of milk. He drank it slowly, and then asked, "How much do I owe you?" "You don't owe me anything," she replied. "Mother has taught us never to accept pay for a kindness."

"Then I thank you from my heart," the boy said. As he left that house, he not only felt stronger physically, but his faith in God and man was also intensified. He had been ready to give up and quit.

Years later, that young woman became critically ill. The local doctors were baffled. They finally sent her to the big city, where they called in specialists to study her rare disease. Dr. Howard Kelly was called in for the consultation. When he heard the name of the town she came from, a strange light filled his eyes. Immediately he rose and went down the hall of the hospital to her room.

Dressed in his doctor's gown he went in to see her. He recognized her at once. He went back to the consultation room determined to do his best to save her life. From that day, he gave special attention to the case. After a long struggle, the battle was won. Dr. Kelly requested the business office to pass the final bill to him for approval.

He looked at it, then wrote something on the edge and the bill was sent to her room. She feared to open it, for she was sure it would take the rest of her life to pay for it all. Finally she looked, and something caught her attention on the side of the bill. She read these words: "Paid in full—with one glass of milk."

Dr. Howard Kelly, once a poor starving boy, was at last able to repay his childhood benefactor!

The moral: There is a divine plan that governs our lives, and those who give will in the end receive.

Message for Tuesday

You can't have it all.

When the historian Doris Kearns Goodwin gave the commencement address to the graduates of Lafayette College in Easton, Pennsylvania, in June 2001, her words had a profound impact on all those present.

She recalled how she ended up working for former President Lyndon Johnson—both in the White House during the last year of his presidency as well as on his ranch for the last four years of his life—to help him with his memoirs.

Here is how she described the final years of a world-famous figure, who enjoyed untold wealth, prestige, and power:

> Now, on the surface, he should have had everything in the world to be grateful for in those last years. His career in politics had reached its peak in becoming President of the United States. He had all the money he needed to pursue

any leisure activity he wanted. He owned a spacious ranch in the country, a penthouse apartment in the city, a half dozen cars equipped with traveling bars, a sailboat, a speedboat, a movie theater in his own home, and this amazing swimming pool that was equipped with floating rafts, on top of which were floating desks and floating notepads and floating sandwiches, so that you could work at every moment.

And yet the man I saw in his retirement had spent so many years in pursuit of work, power, and individual success that he had absolutely no psychic or emotional resources left to commit himself to anything once the presidency was taken from him.

Years of concentration solely on work meant that in his retirement he could find no solace in recreation, sports, or hobbies.

A month before he died, he spoke to me with immense sadness in his voice. He said he was watching the American people absorbed in a new President, forgetting him, forgetting, he feared, even the great civil rights laws that he had passed, and was beginning to think that his quest for immortality had been in vain.

Perhaps, he said, he would have been better off focusing more time and attention on his family.[1]

The Moral: Good fortune doesn't count as much as family. It was too late for President Johnson to learn that lesson, but it's not too late for you.

Message for Wednesday

Where the treasure is hidden.

Many years ago in the great city of Cracow in Poland there lived a very poor Jew named Eisak. He earned his living as a Hebrew teacher. There were many mouths to feed in his family, many bodies to clothe, and always he wondered where he would get the money to provide for them.

One night he dreamed a strange dream, a dream that was to change his entire life. In the far-off city of Prague, he saw a great castle built of wonderful brown stone with many turrets rising up into the sky. Near the castle stretched a bridge, and under the bridge was buried a treasure! At first he paid no attention to the dream. After all, what could such a dream have to do with him? But strangely enough, the very next night he had the exact same dream—in Prague there was a castle, near the castle a bridge, under the bridge was buried a treasure. And the third night the dream returned again. So Eisak began to feel that perhaps the dream was something more than just a dream. Perhaps it was a message from heaven and there really *was* a treasure waiting for him in Prague.

Early the next morning, he packed a small knapsack, put a shovel over his shoulder, bid goodbye to his wife and children, and began the long journey on foot to Prague. When, tired and hungry, he at last approached the outskirts of the city, he raised his eyes to look for the castle—and lo and behold, there it stood, on the highest hill, built of shining brown stone just as he had seen in his dream. He hurried on until he reached a point beneath the bridge, removed his shovel from his shoulder, and was about to begin to dig for the treasure, when he noticed that on the bridge there were guards walking to and fro. He decided it might be wiser to wait until it was night and they had gone home so no one could observe his actions. To his dismay, when night arrived, the day guards were replaced by night guards. So several days of waiting passed until the poor Jew, hungry and exhausted from his long trip, decided to dig for his treasure despite the danger.

When one of the guards saw him digging, he at once came down from the bridge and inquired what he was doing. Frightened by the guard's question, the Jew revealed to him the story of his dream. The guard listened to the tale and then laughed aloud. "That is really funny," he said, "because you see I too have been having a dream every night that I cannot seem to get rid of. It is a foolish dream but I shall tell it to you anyway. I dreamed that in far-off Cracow there lives a Jew, a teacher of Hebrew by the name of Eisak—a strange name, no?—and in the broken-down shack in which he lives is an old stove, and under that stove is buried a treasure! But of course, I don't believe in dreams!''

Eisak listened in silent amazement to the words of the guard. When the latter had finished, he uttered not a word but quickly packed his belongings, put his shovel back over his shoulder and started back for Cracow as fast as his feet could carry him. When he arrived, he made straight for his house, went to the stove, and incredibly enough when he dug underneath it—there was the treasure!

He had traveled many miles, far from home, to seek his wealth. He finally discovered he was running not *to* it, but *from* it—because his true treasure had always been in his own household.

The Moral: We spend our lives running in pursuit of fortune, without realizing that it has always been close at hand, in our very own homes—the one place we never thought to look.

Message for Thursday

It's never too late.

As the great philosopher of our generation, Yogi Berra, once said, "It ain't over till it's over." The true tragedy of life is not that we grow old (think of the alternative); rather, in the words of Robert J. Donovan, "Giving up is the ultimate tragedy."

Can your life still change when you are in your sixties? How about in your seventies, eighties, or nineties? Myrtle Thomas, of Missouri Valley, Iowa, would surely think that's a foolish question.

On her 100th birthday, she received a special present from the University of Nebraska at Omaha: her college diploma.

Myrtle was always bothered because she never got her degree. She lacked sixteen weeks of student teaching, which meant she would have had to give up working for those four months—which she couldn't afford to do. Myrtle made up her mind that she was going to get the dean of the education department to waive the student teaching requirement so that she could get her degree at long last. Yes, she finally succeeded.

Her great grandson, Chad Rotolo, assured her that if she kept working she could probably get her masters degree by age 105. The newspapers reported that she accepted the challenge.

Moral: People are like wine. Age sours the bad and improves the good. The passing of time isn't a curse but a challenge. You're never too old to change your life, your career, your achievements, and your fortune.

Message for Friday

The empty box.

Some time ago, a man punished his three-year-old daughter for wasting a roll of gold wrapping paper. Money was tight and he was furious when the child tried to decorate a box. Nevertheless, the little girl brought the gift to her father the next morning and said, "This is for you, Daddy." He was embarrassed by his earlier overreaction, but his anger flared again when he found the box was empty.

He yelled at her: "Don't you know when you give someone a present, there's supposed to be something inside it?" The little girl looked up at him with tears in her eyes and said, "Oh, Daddy, it's not empty, I blew kisses into the box. All for you, Daddy." The father was crushed. He put his arms around his little girl, and he begged for her forgiveness.

An accident took the life of the child only a short time later and the father kept that gold box by his bed for many years. Whenever he was discouraged, he would take out an imaginary kiss and remember the love of the child who had put it there.

Moral: Open your eyes to really see. Empty boxes can be filled with gifts far more valuable than all the gold in the world.

Message for Saturday

"And this too shall pass."

One day, King Solomon decided to humble Benaiah ben Ye-hoyada, his most trusted minister. He said to him, "Benaiah, there is a certain ring that I want you to bring to me. I wish to wear it for the festival of Sukkot, the holiday of the harvest, which gives you six months to find it."

"If it exists anywhere on earth, your majesty," replied Benaiah, "I will find it and bring it to you. But what makes the ring so special?"

"It has magic powers," answered the king. "If a happy man looks at it, he becomes sad, and if a sad person looks at it, he becomes happy." Solomon knew that no such ring existed in the world, but he wished to give his minister a little taste of humility.

Spring passed and the summer, and still Benaiah had no idea where he could find the ring. On the day before Sukkot, he decided to take a walk in one of the poorest quarters of Jerusalem. He passed by a merchant who had begun to set out the day's wares on a shabby carpet. "Have you by any chance heard of a magic ring that makes the happy wearer forget his joy and the broken-hearted wearer forget his sorrows?" asked Benaiah.

He watched the man take a plain gold ring from his carpet and engrave something on it. When Benaiah read the words on the ring, his face broke out in a wide smile.

That night, the entire city welcomed the holiday of Sukkot with great festivity. "Well, my friend," said Solomon, "have you found what I sent you after?" All the ministers laughed and Solomon himself smiled.

To everyone's surprise, Benaiah held up a small gold ring and declared, "Here it is, your majesty!" And as Solomon read the inscription, the smile vanished from his face. The jeweler had written three Hebrew words on the gold band: *"Gam zu ya'avor—and this too shall pass."*

Abraham Lincoln immortalized this phrase in an address he gave to the Wisconsin State Agricultural Society in 1859. He told the story and then concluded: "How much this thought expresses! How chastening in the hour of pride! How consoling in the depths of affliction!"

Moral: Life is not stagnant. God never promised you a rose garden—nor did He threaten you with a life filled only with thorns and weeds. For those of you who are now suffering, I grant you the gift of Solomon's ring. Look carefully at the word "life" and see that there is a shorter word, "if," at its center. We cannot know what the future holds in store for us. We can be comforted, though, in the times of our depression by the wisdom of these words: "And this too shall pass."

My prayer for you, dear reader, is that just as you have seen joy turn to sorrow, the future will quickly usher in a time when your tears turn to laughter.

Note

1. Doris Kearns Goodwin, "At College Graduations, Wit and Wisdom," *New York Times,* May 28, 2001.

Index